PREPARING THEIR FINAL JOURNEY

On March 26, police discovered an incredible, shocking sight behind the doors of an ornate mansion in the exclusive San Diego community known as Rancho Santa Fe. Twenty women and nineteen men ranging in age from 26 to 72, dressed identically in black and wearing brand-new Nikes, were found lying throughout the three million dollar house on cots and beds. They were all dead, with purple shrouds covering their faces and bodies.

As the horrifying details began to emerge, investigators discovered that they were a self-sufficient cult of computer web page designers, who had chosen to end their lives. Their leader was the charismatic and controversial Marshall Applewhite, known as "Do." a sixties dropout whose obsessive nature drove him to create the Heaven's Gate cult.

In this gripping account of the strange deaths and mysterious lives of the Heaven's Gate members, a team of *New York Post* writers reveals the disturbing truth about a cult that is too close for comfort.

HEAVEN'S GATE CULT SUICIDE IN SAN DIEGO

By the staff of the *New York Post*

Written by

Bill Hoffmann and Cathy Burke

HarperPaperbacks
A Division of HarperCollins*Publishers*

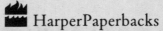

HarperPaperbacks

A Division of HarperCollins*Publishers*
10 East 53rd Street, New York, N.Y. 10022-5299

Copyright © 1997 by the New York Post
All rights reserved. No part of this book may be used or
reproduced in any manner whatsoever without written
permission of the publisher, except in the case of brief
quotations embodied in critical articles and reviews.
For information address HarperCollins*Publishers*,
10 East 53rd Street, New York, N.Y. 10022-5299.

ISBN 0-06-101272-6
MMDI ISBN 0-06-101275-0

HarperCollins®, ®, and HarperPaperbacks™
are trademarks of HarperCollins*Publishers* Inc.

Cover photographs courtesy of AP Photo/WTOL-TV
and KCBS-TV (Applewhite) and
AP Photo/Mark J. Terrill (aerial view).

First printing: April 1997

Printed in the United States of America

Visit HarperPaperbacks on the World Wide Web at
http://www.harpercollins.com

❖ 10 9 8 7 6 5 4 3 2 1

To Vince and the kids, John, Jesse and Zoey.
—Cathy Burke.

To Charlie, Joan and Rafael
on Bedford Street, and Mary in Ireland.
—Bill Hoffmann.

Bill Hoffmann and Cathy Burke would like to acknowledge the following people for the invaluable research and reporting that contributed to the writing of this book.

They include Laura Harris and her staff at *The New York Post* library; Gretchen Viehmann of *The New York Post* photo desk; columnists Andrea Peyser and Steve Dunleavy and Neal Travis; and reporters David K. Li, Brendan Bourne, Allen Salkin, Andy Soltis, Tracy Connor, Andy Geller, John O'Mahony, Laura Italiano, Angela Mosconi, Eric Stirgus, Devlin Barrett, Linda Massarella, Dareh Gregorian, Kieran Crowley, Rita Delfiner, Chris Francescani, Mark Morri, Gersh Kuntzman, Maggie Haberman, Lillian Acosta and Jason Chau. Thanks as well to Lou Lumenick and Allen Salkin for their wisdom of the web.

We also are grateful to *New York Post* metropolitan editor Stuart Marques, who chose us to write the book, organized it and did the first edit.

The following publications, newspapers, news services, broadcasters and books also were used in the compilation of material for the book: *The New York Times*, *The New York Times Magazine*, *The Chicago Tribune*, *The Washington Post*, *The Cincinnati Enquirer*, *The*

Albuquerque Tribune, The Dallas News Tribune, The Denver Post, The San Francisco Examiner, The Los Angeles Times, The Boston Herald, The Boston Globe, Newsday, The San Diego Union-Tribune, The Houston Chronicle, The Salt Lake Tribune, Knight-Ridder Newspapers, The Times of London, The Associated Press, Reuter, Scripps-Howard News Service, *The New York Daily News,* Cable News Network, CBS, MSNBC, Fox News Channel, King World, *Psychology Today, Time, Newsweek,* "Waiting for the Ships: Disillusionment and the Revitalization of Faith in Bo and Peep's UFO Cult," an article in *The Gods Have Landed: New Religions From Other Worlds,* edited by James R. Lewis, *The World Almanac and The Psychotronic Video Guide,* by Michael J. Weldon.

We would also like to thank the hard-working people of HarperCollins who turned on a dime to make this happen, including our editor Jessica Lichtenstein, Paul Banks, Julie Blattberg, Kelly Chian, Alan Fergurson, Carl Galian, Tom Finnegan, Leonida Karpik, Randy Sloan, Rebecca Springer, and Amy Wasserman.

And of course our first reader Jan Constantine of News America Publishing.

Table of Contents

HEAVEN'S GATE
CULT SUICIDE IN SAN DIEGO

Chapter

1

THE HOUSE AT 18241 COLINA NORTE

Nick Matzorkis waited tensely outside the sprawling Spanish-style mansion ringed with palm trees, a swimming pool and tennis courts. He waited and stared at the large white front door his friend Robert "Rio" D'Angelo had walked through just two minutes earlier.

It was a warm, breezy day, with temperatures hovering around seventy degrees—perfect for a stroll, a bike ride, a drive with the top down. It was the start of spring and another beautiful day in southern California.

But Matzorkis didn't seem to notice, keeping his eyes rigidly trained on the door for signs of his friend Rio instead. Groups of black flies buzzed around the entrance.

That's odd, he thought.

As president of a successful Beverly Hills software company called Interact Entertainment Group, the thirty-four-year-old businessman was usually in his office at this hour, making deals, taking calls, speaking with his executives about projects.

To be standing outside a large, seemingly empty mansion with a distant view of the Pacific, some two hours from downtown Los Angeles, seemed sort of like cutting classes.

And yet, he had agreed to make this unusual journey at the behest of Rio D'Angelo, a gifted employee and former member of a computer-obsessed religious cult known as "Heaven's Gate."

Matzorkis—whose deep-set eyes, receding hairline and pointed chin gave him the dashing look of actor Stanley Tucci—had met a few of its members through Rio but didn't know a great deal about the cult.

Rio, forty-one, had set up a business arrangement between Heaven's Gate and Interact to produce some websites.

Just four months earlier, Matzorkis had watched in amusement as several of the cult members surprised him at his office with a chocolate birthday cake.

It was a relaxed event with cultists quietly talking about the Internet and the vast potential it had to help promote their beliefs. Then one of the women who had carried the cake said something in passing that gave him a jolt.

"You know," she said nonchalantly, "several of the male members had undergone surgery to have their testicles removed!" In other words, voluntary castration. Jesus, eunuchs!

Matzorkis uneasily glanced across the room at the male faces before him, speculating on which ones might be without their "balls."

Then it hit him—a remark he'd heard months earlier but had paid little attention to. One of the cultists had insisted that all members of Heaven's Gate were celibate—no sex whatsoever was allowed among cult members. Hmmm, a likely story. Weren't most cults, rife with stories of free love, wild sex orgies, and multiple partners?

It all seemed to make more sense now as Matzorkis surveyed the gathering. Everybody appeared androgynous with extremely short hair and loose dark pants and shirts.

Most of the women seemed to have very small breasts, when you could see traces of them at all. And from the back, they all pretty much looked the same.

And all of them, well educated with a full command of the language, seemed to have an extraordinary interest in science fiction—particularly in *Star Trek* and The *X-Files.*

After the birthday surprise, Matzorkis would get periodic letters or phone calls from a cult member. Once he received an e-mail message asking if he would be interested in helping produce a movie about Heaven's Gate and its beliefs.

The computer company president didn't have to think long before begging off. Certainly there were stranger, more compelling stories out there than what this group had to offer.

"I remember them expressing frustration that in over twenty years of the group's existence they had been unable to draw attention to themselves," Matzorkis would recall later.

He was equally unimpressed at the group's attempt to produce a short video about itself called, "Planet About to be Recycled: Your Only Chance to Survive, Leave with Us," which came with a cover letter stating:

> "Think of us as an away team from space—a captain and his crew— making a last attempt just before their departure to inform Earth's inhabitants of the only solution to their predicament of being enslaved by malevolent space aliens."

Heaven's Gate and its wacky "no-sex-please" brood was a distant thought in Matzorkis' mind on the morning of March 26, as he sat in his office going over contracts. That's when Rio burst in, clutching two videocassettes and a letter.

The handwritten note said, matter-of-factly: "By the time this is read, we will have shed our containers. . . . We suspect the human bodies we were wearing have been found. We'll be gone. We came from the Level Above Human in distant space and we now have exited the bodies that we were wearing for our earthly task."

It sounded like a line from a bad science-fiction movie. But the contents of the two videotapes showed some of the people he'd once called brothers and sisters in the Heaven's Gate cult giving short farewell speeches, quietly and without much emotion.

Rio and Matzorkis watched them in disbelief.

Paired off in two's and sitting on plastic lawn chairs, the cultists, all dressed in dark, similar clothing, rattled off what seemed like prepared good-byes to friends and family.

"I'm about to take an act that probably to anyone in this world would seem to be the most horrible thing anyone could do," one man explained, staring into the camera.

"This will bring me just the happiest day of my life. I've been looking forward to this for so long," another man said.

A twenty-something woman with close-cropped brown hair and gentle green eyes, beamed as she explained: "We are all choosing of our own free will to go to the next level."

On and on they went. The finality of their statements impressed—and chilled—both men.

One man wearing wire-rimmed spectacles and a black turtleneck, said: "If humans were told about the truth about what was going on on this planet, they'd be shocked and wouldn't continue in their eight-to-five slavery and ignorance."

"If you could just get into our head space a little bit," added one man in his late thirties.

As the tape went on, it was evident that there were two possibilities of what it all meant. Either this was one really bad exercise in science fiction, possibly the cult's warped idea of a pilot for the show they had wanted to make about themselves. Or it meant something far more serious—that this group was about to take some drastic step. It sounded as if they were about to kill themselves.

Two of the more emotional speakers basically spelled the latter theory out.

"You know," one middle-aged woman with aviator glasses began, "we are like vehicles. I mean if you use the analogy of a car and, you know, people may keep their cars for a long time before they finally wear out and conk out and they die on 'em and, you know, they go and get another car. I mean that's all we're talking about. It's not a big deal."

Oddly, a few of the speakers made mention of two people whose names sounded like fairy tale characters.

"I just want to say how thankful I am to Do and Ti for helping me and taking me under their wing and showing me the ways of the next level. . . . I'm just very thankful for that and I'm trying not to be too serious or emotional here," one woman said.

And finally: "I think everyone . . . wanted something more than this human world had to offer."

Each speaker tried to end on an upbeat note, as if to say, while you may not understand this now, you'll eventually get the picture.

The tapes and the letter, sent by way of Federal Express the day before, gave Rio an uneasy feeling. Subsequent attempts to reach cult members by phone failed.

Rio, worried that something might be terribly wrong, asked Matzorkis to accompany him on a check of the estate the cult had called home since last October.

And now, here they were.

Or at least, here he was, with his buddy Rio inside somewhere doing God knows what.

Another minute passed and Matzorkis began wondering if maybe he should go in search of his missing pal.

Then Rio emerged—looking as grim and as lifeless as a ghost.

His arms hung at his sides, his hands shook. His face was drained of all color. His mouth hung open. He seemed unable to speak, unable to describe what he had just seen inside the house.

"He was as white as a sheet," Matzorkis recalled.

Rio breathlessly mumbled a few words and the pair sped off to notify authorities.

At 3:30 P.M., the San Diego County Sheriff's Department answered a 911 call.

"There has been a mass suicide at 18241 Colina Norte," an excited voice blurted out. The caller would not identify himself.

The statement startled the dispatcher, who, when it came to taking emergency calls from the Colina Norte area, was more used to hearing about heart attacks, domestic disputes and lost pets.

Colina Norte, is, after all, located in the heart of Rancho Santa Fe, which is proudly known to the locals as "The Beverly Hills of San Diego" and also "The Ranch."

Mass suicide? As the dispatcher notified a manned radio car to respond to the scene, deputies who had overheard the complaint were skeptical it could be anything more than a crank call.

People certainly didn't kill themselves like lemmings over cliffs in Rancho Santa Fe, one of the wealthiest communities in the southwestern United States.

A community of 1,800 homes and estates which proudly boasted that it has one of the nation's most perfect climates with dry, but not arid air, and a tolerable humidity.

Nestled in picturesque hills that separate the Pacific from the California desert,

Rancho Santa Fe has always been associated with beautiful things—including its name.

Translated from Spanish, Rancho Santa Fe means "Saint Faith."

And set amid lush, rolling hills dotted by eucalyptus and citrus trees, the lush community certainly lives up to its name as a place of faith that was fit for a saint.

Populated by sprawling million-dollar homes with neatly fenced horse pastures, swimming pools, private tennis courts, and putting greens, Rancho Santa Fe has also established itself as a playground of the rich and famous.

In terms of wealth, it is a sort of West Coast version of Palm Beach without the sleazy scandals.

Rancho Santa Fe had developed quickly, thanks to the growth of Hollywood in the '20s, as well as the stock boom which created millionaires out of businessmen, politicians and lawyers who played the market.

It was particularly embraced by Hollywood which had earned the title of "Motion Picture Capital of the World" with its scores of silent film stars who grinded out comedies,

swashbuckling adventures and tearjerking
romances to the delight of millions.

But while Hollywood in its golden age had
an undeniable creative energy, its talent
found it tiring. They fled the unending hustle
and bustle and fast-con world of Los Angeles
for the peace and tranquillity of country
homes by the sea in Rancho Santa Fe.

They realized that outside of Beverly
Hills, which was just too close to work,
Rancho Santa Fe provided the best their
money could buy. It not only lacked the
crime, the corruption, and the kookiness of
Tinseltown, but it was a mere two-hour
drive.

Debonair actor Douglas Fairbanks Jr.,
whose dad had made his fortune grinding
out flicks like *The Black Pirate*, called it "the
most beautiful place I have ever lived," as
did Victor Mature, whose red Rolls Royce
golf cart was a familiar sight for years.

Silent screen sweetheart Mary Pickford
never wanted to leave her home in Rancho
Santa Fe and longtime Miss America host
Bert Parks and "Tennessee Waltz" warbler
Patti Page also swore by it.

Robert Young of *Father Knows Best* and

Marcus Welby, M.D. fame, noted that Rancho Santa Fe was the perfect antidote for the madness of La-La Land.

Pete Rozelle, the late NFL Commissioner, and Neil Regan, the late brother of the former president were also longtime residents.

The list of homeowners remains a Who's Who of the nation's biggest movers and shakers to this day.

Mercury astronaut Wally Schirra told friends the only place that topped the beauty of Rancho Santa Fe was the out-of-this-world view of Planet Earth from his space capsule.

Cop-turned-bestselling author Joseph Wambaugh and San Diego Padres owner John Moores found Rancho Santa Fe the perfect complement to their frantic schedules.

Even rock 'n' roll's next generation of alternative stars latched on, led by chart-topping singer Jewel who bought an estate, telling friends she'd found her slice of heaven.

In the mid '30s, Bing Crosby brought worldwide prominence to the community by launching his Bing Crosby Pro/Am Golf Tournament there.

"Der Bingle" reluctantly would be forced to move the gala, star-studded event to Pebble Beach when it grew too big for "The Ranch."

Despite that loss, the area remained the number-one destination for those planning tennis vacations. Horse trainers also found that it had the ideal climate for raising and training thoroughbreds such as Cigar.

The unbridled charm of Rancho Santa Fe is a tribute to planning because the area stands as the oldest planned community in California. Founded in 1928 out of an unincorporated area of San Diego, the town was financed by the Santa Fe Railroad.

The size of the average property was penciled into the planning books as three acres.

Year by year, the median income of residents grew steadily as did property values with the latest median income being $93,000 and the average home going for about $1.3 million.

The median income and property values steadily grew thanks to a rigid set of rules which for nearly seventy years restricted exactly what can be built, what it can look like and how big it can be.

Under a so-called "zoning covenant"—a document that has been challenged over and over but never overruled—homeowners and builders must submit plans for any and all changes they want to make.

Changes from the simplest roofing job, to the installation of exterior lighting, to the planting of certain types of shrubs and flowers all must go before a special zoning commission—*no* exceptions.

"The covenant is a love-hate situation," explained businessman Rae Mowery.

"It says, 'No, no, no, you can't do this or that,' but it controls your neighbor for your benefit. It has worked very well."

All houses must conform to a Mediterranean or early California style—retro architecture which some residents believed the house at the end of a cul-de-sac, at 18241 Colina Norte, had only partially lived up to.

The two-story cream-colored, Spanish mansion located on three rolling acres on a hill twenty miles north of San Diego, is a weird hybrid between a monastery and an upscale, retro condo.

Directly behind the 9,300 square-foot

residence, with its nine bedrooms and
seven and a half baths, is a large in-ground
swimming pool, a regulation-size Har-Tru
tennis court, and a modest putting green.

Surrounding both is a lush orchard of
fruit trees yielding edible lemons, avocados,
juice oranges, and pink grapefruits. Without
a doubt, it could be described as an uncomfortable union of the big and the beautiful
and the ghastly and the gawdy.

But even the fussiest of critics couldn't
say a word against the views: sweeping and
commanding panoramas of the Pacific
Ocean and surrounding canyon.

Those attributes alone made the boast in
one real-estate magazine that the residence
is one of "San Diego's greatest dream
homes" almost unchallengable.

The two sheriff's deputies who had been
contacted by headquarters to respond to the
house, flicked on their emergency lights
and blasted their siren to alert traffic on
their five-minute trip up the hill.

Whether this 911 report of a "mass suicide" was true, neither could say. But it got

them thinking about the strange and tragic history of the fourteen-year-old residence that locals had gossiped about for years.

The previous owners, financier Robert Ferrier and his wife, Maria Nixon, bought the place in 1985 and moved lock, stock and barrel from New Jersey to California with only one thing in mind: to save the life of their severely-crippled daughter.

Lisa Ferrier had the healthy pink blush of any healthy little baby when she was born in 1977. But soon it was determined that she was afflicted with cerebral palsy.

As the disease grew worse, little Lisa's legs and arms curled and twisted into odd positions, her speech became partially unintelligible and she began to endure intense and unending pain.

Treatments in New York City's top hospitals could do nothing. The Ferriers were told the only help they could truly give Lisa was a year-round warm climate, which would ease her pain and possibly prolong her life.

The family moved into the home in 1986 after Lisa turned nine and Maria Nixon immediately went about making the ritzy structure into a showcase for handicapped access.

She made every entrance accessible by wheelchair, installed an elevator to the second floor and even turned one room into a mini-medical center in case of emergencies.

Neighbors recalled how Lisa would sit in her wheelchair by the pool and watch different varieties of birds effortlessly flap from the fruit trees to the rose bushes to the palm plants, and sometimes burst into tears.

But Lisa had many good times, too, and seemed to relish the seemingly endless days of cloudless skies, particularly when she heard about the blizzards and thunderstorms she'd been used to in her old home in the Northeast.

"It was the nicest place you could think of to grow up in," recalled Lisa's brother, Richard Ferrier.

Lisa's condition began deteriorating in 1993 to the point that she left the house less and less and within a year she succumbed to the disease.

Her death devastated her parents, who were so emotionally ravaged by their daughter's eight-year-struggle that their marriage disintegrated.

They divorced just months after Lisa's funeral and sold the house three years ago to a forty-five-year-old businessman named Sam Koutchesfahani, owner of a business in San Diego called Tan Trading and Consulting Group.

Within a year, Koutchesfahani had his own cross to bear: the scrutiny of the Internal Revenue Service and the San Diego district attorney's office.

Koutchesfahani, pleaded guilty to tax evasion and fraud charges last year after admitting he had made about $350,000 from Middle Eastern students between 1989 and 1995.

Prosecutors said Koutchesfahani used the money to bribe college instructors at three San Diego area colleges—San Diego City, Mesa, and Palomar—into illegally enrolling students and certifying them as California residents.

Authorities also believed—although never proved—that Koutchesfahani sold counterfeit degrees, GED certificates, and "California resident" documents used by college students.

Koutchesfahani stayed out of jail, but

found his monthly upkeep and mortgage payments on the property impossible to meet.

The solution, he realized, was sell—and fast. The problem was that with a solid but sluggish market, the sale was going to take a while, certainly more time than the financially troubled businessman had.

His other option was renting the property out for a sum that would cover his mortgage and expenses and provide a couple extra hundred in spending money for himself.

Koutchesfahani advertised the property, and within two weeks a local real estate agency had provided an eager, and what seemed like an ideal, tenant: a Christian group calling itself "Heaven's Gate."

A cult? Maybe. A little bit wacky. Probably. But one which had a clear thought on one key issue. Members had absolutely no problem in paying the hefty monthly rental of $7,200.

What's more, the group of what seemed like a bunch of very plain Janes and the most ordinary of Joes had a spotless referral letter from a doctor who had once rented them his home in nearby Fairbanks Ranch.

So what if they had chosen the title of what was considered the biggest bomb in movie history to name themselves after? So what if they weren't exactly fashion plates? The only color that made a difference in Sam's eyes was green—for cash.

And cash was what they paid, because none of the cultists believed in checkbooks.

In late September 1996, two representatives from Heaven's Gate emerged to seal the deal—a bald, blue-eyed man in his seventies who identified himself only as "Father John" and a younger, bookish assistant named "Brother Logan."

They were quiet, humble, and respectful with none of the aura of the tenant that homeowners fear the most: the careless, let's-party-baby type of renters who tend to wreck havoc in the nicest of homes.

In fact, as delighted neighborhood kids would tell their parents, Father John kind of resembled "Lurch" the ghoulish seven-foot servant played by actor Ted Cassidy on TV's *Addams Family*.

With serious and convincing authority, Father John and Brother Logan explained that Heaven's Gate consisted of a reverent group of living angels who had been sent to Earth to help mankind.

John and Logan said their flock had come together in the Midwest over a decade earlier and had doggedly traveled the country spreading the word.

While their beliefs and goals weren't exactly his cup of tea, Koutchesfahani had no problem with what he heard. In fact, some of it sounded like downright common sense.

"They expressed to Sam that they didn't believe in the government—not in the anti-government Oklahoma City type sense but in the religious sense," Koutchesfahani's lawyer Milton Silverman said.

"They believed that there is a spiritual world and a secular world and that the government had no right to stamp a number on them—to assign a Social Security number."

But Silverman said neither he nor his client considered the Heaven's Gate group to be wackos.

"They did not live like a bunch of crazy people and they kept the place immaculate," Silverman said.

The goodwill extended by the group included members repainting and redecorating every room in the house, refinishing wood trim and mowing the lawn—all without asking for a reduction in rent, a landlord's dream.

Members of Heaven's Gate seemed to live conservatively for all Sam could tell—lights out early, simple meals and few functions outside.

The only extravagance appeared to be a whopping monthly phone bill of about $1,000 a month—with many of those calls to European countries. The phone bills came to Koutchesfahani, who inspected them, then passed them on to his tenants.

During one conversation, Koutchesfahani felt so comfortable with his tenants, he even confided in them about his problems with the law.

Father John, Brother Logan, and others commiserated, gave their landlord religious literature to read and donated a computer to his son.

"He liked these people," Silverman recalled.

One neighbor on the block who wished to remain anonymous said there was one very solid reason why landlord and tenant got along so well.

In light of Koutchesfahani's tax plea, the Heaven's Gate group "cheerfully admitted that they didn't like paying taxes either. They were against it all the way."

Koutchesfahani didn't appear to mind that people knew he was renting the house to a group of apparent religious conservatives.

When one neighbor asked him his plans for the estate, he joked: "I can't sell it right now. I'm renting to a bunch of monks."

Koutchesfahani may have taken his tenants lightly. On the other hand, San Diego's real-estate agents, who were trying to push a sale of the residence for a hefty commission, did not.

Showing the gigantic luxury home at the end of the long, snaking driveway was always a challenge—often one with unforeseen obstacles.

For one thing, the authoritative Brother Logan always restricted access to the property to one single four-hour period, one day a week. He didn't say why the place was off-limits the rest of the time and the real-estate people had no chance to argue. The property was heavily gated and almost impossible to enter unless you were willing to risk life and limb climbing over.

Making matters worse, prospective buyers found it hard to take their eyes off the always looming Logan, and often rushed through the tour.

Even when brokers fit their clients into Brother Logan's four-hour window, it was always a struggle to make the right presentation because of how the Heaven's Gate people had furnished the interior. "Weird" was one word often used.

Each bedroom contained metal-frame bunkbeds and desktop computers—making the inside appear more like a college dorm than a so-called dream house.

The living room had almost no furniture—except for a giant-screen TV flanked by huge stereo speakers.

On the large fireplace mantel was a stark, framed drawing of an extraterrestrial—one not unlike the aliens seen in Steven Spielberg's science-fiction hit, *Close Encounters of the Third Kind*.

Underneath the drawing was a handwritten

explanation, reading: "A member of the next level."

One real-estate agent remarked that the stark metal bunks, computers and TV screen made the place seem like an "earthbound spaceship."

Brother Logan and his brood smiled when they heard about the remark and seemed to approve of it.

In fact, he told several real-estate agents with a touching sincerity, the home *was* their "ship."

"This is nothing more than a temporary stop as we journey back to our home base," Brother Logan explained.

He went on. To get to their real home in outer space, the members of Heaven's Gate would leave their "human bodies" behind on Earth.

Members would become extraterrestrials before they died and were lifted off to heaven, he explained.

While it sounded like mumbo-jumbo, like a fantastic scenario out of an *Outer Limits* episode, members were quick to explain that it wasn't that far removed from Roman Catholicism or other mainstream religions.

After all, they reckoned, the Christian belief is that the soul lives forever, leaving the physical body after it expires. So, what's so different about us, they asked.

As wacked-out as their talk of space beings and body-shedding might have been, nobody in the neighborhood besides real-estate agents really knew about the claims, simply because the group was quiet.

San Diego police had never been called to the mansion before.

Because Rancho Santa Fe is the home to an estimated five percent of the nation's millionaires, it is a place where residents are well accustomed to eccentric characters.

So even when the occasional rumors floated around town about the "bunch of religious weirdos living up on the hill" nobody batted an eyelash.

Still, real-estate agent Marvin Caldwell and a partner couldn't forget their uneasy encounter with Logan and a dozen other cult members at a small estate sale the group held.

"He said they were selling the stuff because they were planning on moving," Caldwell said.

"He said they were preparing to take a long journey."

The group members would slip by describing how they were going to another ship—then catch themselves and adjust the word "ship" to "home."

Scott Warren of Dyson and Dyson Real Estate Associates remembered Brother Logan and his followers as "a little strange."

"That can mean anything in Rancho Santa Fe," he said. "There are a lot of people with a lot of money, and they can be a little eccentric, or decorate things a little differently."

Logan "was definitely in charge. He was very cordial but very intimidating. He had a heavy presence," Warren remembered.

The leader asked them to take off their shoes and slip on cotton surgical booties.

"He asked us to take off our shoes because they were a religious group and shoes were contaminating," Warren said.

He led the startled group into the living room with its sixty-inch TV and computers.

One room featured a ballet barre and mirrors. Inside, a small army of people typed away at dozens of computers—

"working like little worker bees," Warren recalled.

The "worker bees," several agents recalled, looked a bit like factory workers out of one of those "red scare" propaganda movies from the '50s.

Each wore loose, drabbly colored clothing which covered their figures and hid all body parts except their heads and hands.

All of the bedrooms, too, had computers and most had shelves of books. Some were factual science manuals and nonfiction books about space, while others were popular science-fiction novels and tales of fantasy.

The visitors were never left alone in any of the rooms, even for a few seconds. One of the occupants explained their concern about who was inside the house by noting, "This is our temple."

"It was definitely weird," Warren said. "But I've been in real estate for twenty years, and you see a lot of weird stuff."

Real-estate agent Caldwell recalled: "Every morning, Brother Logan told us, they got up at four A.M., got their telescope, and looked at their home star in the northeast sky. To him, it was not a spiritual experience. He was looking at his home."

How long this bizarre group was planning to stay was anybody's guess. But real-estate firms knew there was little chance of selling the place with its current inhabitants always in evidence.

One agent got the feeling that something was about to give. Exactly what, he did not know.

As the two deputy sheriffs rounded the first curve of the long and winding road to the house at 18241 Colina Norte, several neighborhood kids stopped playing in their yards to watch. What was going on?

While wealth has certainly sheltered Rancho Santa Fe from a lot of the crime and lurid activities that affect much less affluent communities, "The Ranch" had a few notorious moments of shocking violence and mayhem on its resume.

The community had been rocked four years ago by a mind-numbing murder-suicide that made headlines around the world.

Ian Spiro, a prominent British businessman who worked for both the CIA and the British secret service, shot his wife and three young children in November 1992 in their rented million-dollar home.

Spiro—despondent and depressed because he was heavily in debt—then sat with his family's bodies for three days.

When the stench of the rotting corpses began to overwhelm the house and concerned neighbors who had not seen the family began banging on the door, Spiro reached for a bag of capsules in his pocket.

He chewed several pills laced with cyanide and collapsed dead next to his murdered wife and kids. The family was subsequently found to be five million dollars in debt.

One of the worst air crashes in American history occurred not far from Rancho Santa Fe in 1978 when a commercial passenger jet approaching San Diego airport was struck in mid-air by a small Cessna.

All 144 people on board both aircraft perished and seven people on the ground were killed by tons of falling debris.

In 1979, a sixteen-year-old girl shot and

killed an elementary school principal, a jan-
itor and eight children in the neighboring
suburb of San Carlos with a rifle she had
received as a Christmas present.

Perhaps the worst slaughter occurred in
nearby San Ysidro, when James Huberty,
forty-one, marched into a crowded
McDonald's restaurant on July 18, 1984
and, without saying a word, opened fire.

Huberty blew away twenty people before
police sharpshooters cut him down. The
McDonald's Corporation was so rattled by
the massacre, it tore down the fast-food
eatery and replaced it with a park in memory of the victims.

In 1989 postal worker John Taylor shot
and killed his wife and two co-workers,
killing himself a day later.

Four years later, a nineteen-year-old college student opened fire in a family fitness
center in El Cajon, killing four people
before blowing his brains out. And two
years ago, a deranged man murdered five
members of his family with a hammer, a
knife, and an axe in the suburb of Vista
before torching the house to try to cover up
his murderous rage. He later confessed.

▽   ▽   ▽

Sam Koutchesfahani's house seemed strangely quiet as the sheriff's patrol car pulled into the circular driveway and Deputies Robert Brunk and Laura Gacek began a visual inspection of the property. Odd that on such a perfect day not a soul was outside doing chores, cutting the grass, gardening, anything.

The police had not been ignorant of the cult members' comings and goings since taking up residence "up on the hill" last October.

Every two weeks, almost like clockwork, three of the cultists—two women and one man wearing identical light blue pants and white shirts and sporting crewcuts—drove their red Chevy van into town and entered the popular Original Pancake House.

In a town where Brooks Brothers, Donna Karan, and Calvin Klein are the norm in fashion, this trio looked positively bizarre and drew endless stares from the heavily preppie crowd.

The twice-a-month ritual appeared to be a treat for the cultists who ordered a stack of strawberry pancakes each visit.

The waitresses soon learned to hold the standard order of coffee for the trio when they informed them that they never consumed caffeine. The drink of choice was herbal tea—one cup, no more, no less.

"They were really polite—they always said please and thank you and were soft-spoken," waitress Robyn Ketchum recalled.

The man seemed to be the leader and would leave as much as a twenty-five percent tip each visit, she remembered.

One time they asked to leave their van in the parking lot to go off on a "retreat." The trio didn't return to pick up their vehicle for an entire week and then offered little information about where they had been.

Other members—similarly dressed—occasionally were seen at a local cybercafe called Gigabytes where they would promote their group and its computer website called "Higher Source."

In a wealthy town where high-priced fashions are supposed to show off curves, promote sexy bodies and make less than perfect figures seem terrific, the Heaven's Gate crowd stood out for their complete lack of showmanship.

With their baggy clothes and short hair, they all appeared androgynous. Hips didn't matter, the outline of the breast was inconsequential.

Whereas some oddball cults attracted rumors of wild sex orgies and S&M sessions, the buzz on Heaven's Gate was the opposite. Celibacy and teetotaling were in, at least that's what they told their landlord and others.

Eric Morales, a waiter at the Marie Callender restaurant in Carlsbad, seven miles from the "Heaven's Gate" compound in Rancho Santa Fe, was a bit surprised when he saw thirty-nine similarly dressed men and women with short hair quietly march into his eatery on March 21.

He was amused when the leader of the group ordered thirty-nine chicken pot pies, thirty-nine salads with tomato vinaigrette, and thirty-nine iced tea drinks with lemon slices.

"I got the feeling something special was going on. They were very neat and polite and said thank you for every little thing," he remembered.

When the meal ended one woman took out a wad of cash and paid the check for $351—

plus a $52 tip. As the group stood to leave they each passed Morales and shook his hand as if they were about to go off on a journey.

"I did sense something was up," recalled Morales, who got a weird response when he asked them to come back soon. "They just kind of shrugged it off."

Deputies Brunk and Gacek opened the doors of their cruiser and made a quick surveillance of the entranceway to the large home.

The door was closed and nothing seemed amiss. The bright sun had raised the temperature by a few degrees and the carefully manicured property glowed in the sunlight like a golden Eden. What was wrong here? Neither knew—but there was just something not right. Something.

The two officers instinctively radioed to headquarters, requested backup, and then cautiously walked toward the front door.

Brunk carefully reached out, twisted the knob, and pushed open the door.

He didn't know it at the time, but he was about to unleash one of the most bizarre and disturbing chapters in modern American history.

Chapter

2

BEDS, BODIES, AND COMPUTERS

There was no warning for what was coming.

Even with his six years on the force, Deputy Sheriff Robert Brunk couldn't have been prepared for this.

Next to him was his partner Laura Gacek. They stood outside the front door entrance to the hillside house.

They were now seconds away from learning whether that odd 911 call which had been phoned in anonymously was indeed true or a prank.

Brunk flashed his partner a quick look and then carefully reached for the door-knob.

He turned it and pushed open the door.

In a split second, it slammed into them like some foul, unstoppable creature. A sucker punch of the overpowering smell of death. The horrifying odor was instantly everywhere, blasting their bodies like a wind from hell. It pummeled their nostrils, whipped into their eyes and reached down their throats and into their lungs.

Both officers instantly stepped backward as the heavy gaseous odors of decaying human flesh and internal organs blew out of the house as if being propelled by a fan on full blast.

"Whew!" Gacek said, whacking her hand to her nose to see if it was still there as the stench continued to wreck havoc with her senses.

Both officers had experienced that all-too-familiar, all-too-nauseating odor before—the smell of death, the smell of human flesh decaying. But this was something else, something more, something a hundred times worse than walking past a fully-loaded garbage truck on a hot day. Something almost . . . *inhuman*.

After only a few seconds of exposure to

the rancid and putrid air, both cops were dazed—their eyes on fire, their stunned stomachs churning in horror.

But they had to get inside, to see what was going on. What was in there? Just who was dead, and who, if by any small miracle, might still be alive?

One thing their combined dozen years on the force made them realize instantly was that there was no question this place probably contained a large number of dead people.

And some of them had apparently been dead for awhile.

Brunk and Gacek, their faces nearly drained of color, stepped back, took deep gulps of fresh air, then covered their faces with white cotton surgical masks they had brought along as standard procedure.

They slowly walked into the darkened foyer of the mansion on the hill.

The first thing that hit them was how eerily still the house was. No sound. No sense that anybody lived there. Adding to the creepy ambiance was the occasional distant chirping of birds from outside. But that was it. Nothing else.

The little light that illuminated the place peeked in from the corners of heavy shades which covered the windows. The deputies flicked on a nearby light switch and immediately could see flies buzzing furiously around the living room.

There was no furniture in the living room, except for a few folding chairs and a small table with a clock showing the correct time. The place was nearly devoid of color—everything seemed either off-white or gray. Even the chocolate brown carpeting seemed washed out.

They moved past the living room and into the den.

They froze at the sight of a body with what appeared to be a diamond-shaped purple sheet over it.

The corpse lay on a small Army cot, stretched out ramrod straight from head to toe. The lower half of the corpse was dressed in black pants, dark socks and brand new sneakers. Black and white Nikes with not so much as a scuff on the soles. From the waist to the top of the head the body was blanketed by a rich purple sheet, neatly folded to resemble a large diamond, the points ending at the corpse's groin and crown of the head.

Brunk and Gacek, taking short gulps of air through their masks to lessen the force of the putrid odor, moved on.

They walked into a bedroom off the den. One, two, three, four. Four bodies.

They lay in two metallic bunk beds, in the exact same positions as the first. From the doorway, the place looked like a spacious morgue in which the refrigeration had gone bad.

"It was calm, it was disturbing, it was surreal," Gacek recalled later.

The two sergeants wandered up the carpeted staircase to the second floor and saw from a distance a bedroom with more bunk beds. From their vantage point, they could see feet—again in sneakers—sticking out over the edges of the mattresses.

They had already counted about ten bodies. That was enough for the time being. There was nobody alive in this house, that was for sure. This place was a tomb and as they stood there deciding what to do next, the gases from the decomposing corpses continued to pound

their senses. They knew they had to get
out and let backup take over.

Brunk and Gacek, as are all cops in the
police academy, were taught how to separate the job from human emotion—just as
coroners did when they examined dead
bodies. But the sights here were overpowering. They knew they hadn't seen everything in the house yet but . . .

Then they started to sway. Woozy. We
have to get out fast, they thought. Very
fast.

The lack of fresh air, the overwhelming presence of sickly fumes from the
rotting bodies had them ready to keel
over. They did a reflexive about-face and
moved quickly through the maze of
death, looking for the front door—the
exit back into the world of light, of
sound, of the living.

Brunk and Gacek made it out, both of
them choking for air and moving to sit
down so they could recover their damaged
equilibrium. They began heaving and
coughing heavily. Two more radio cars
pulled up along with an ambulance.
Emergency Services workers checked the

downed pair and were worried, not exactly sure just what they had inhaled in this place.

"Don't go in there, don't go in there without a ventilator," the backup cops were warned.

Placing Brunk and Gacek on stretchers, the attendants rushed them off to the hospital. In the emergency room, tubes of blood were extracted from each officer to determine just how much toxic gas they had inhaled. The doctors on duty listened in horror as the two stunned cops told in fragmented bits and pieces, just what they had witnessed. The hospital staff knew then it was going to be a hell of a long night.

A half-hour later there was a widely circulated report that both sheriff's deputies were in critical condition—with their lungs severely injured by high levels of toxicity in the fumes emitted by the rotting bodies.

The report was wrong. Both officers, it turned out, were expected to recover without any long term physical effects. The psychological effects were another matter. Under sheriff's department policy, the downed cops were visited by a staff psychiatrist who spoke at length with them, to determine whether they needed a leave to recover from the madness they had discovered.

For the next few hours, nobody would enter the house of death as authorities awaited a search warrant and geared up with gas masks and breathing equipment.

A hazardous materials team was dispatched to the scene to help decrease the level of nauseating toxic fumes seeping from the house.

Investigators had a hunch about what lay in waiting for them: a terrible mass suicide, one that would promise to have the hungry media swarming into San Diego from every corner of the globe.

After Deputies Gacek and Brunk had recovered from their respiratory trauma, they reflected on what was to be the most upsetting and bizarre scene of their careers.

Gacek said as soon as the door was opened, she had some idea of what to expect, but was bowled over as she proceeded.

"We just didn't know the magnitude, how many bodies or what condition they were going to be in," Gacek said.

"It was calm, it was disturbing, it was surreal."

Around six P.M. (California time), San Diego police issued a bulletin on the stunning find. The Associated Press ran it as an "URGENT" a short time later:

> RANCHO SANTA FE, Calif. March 26 (AP)—Sheriff's deputies responding to an anonymous call stumbled on a mass suicide at a multi-million dollar mansion Wednesday.

Newsrooms across America began to buzz as more bulletins followed. First there was word that ten bodies had been found. That was quickly changed to "at least ten."

Immediately, reporters and photographers from more than six hundred news organizations around the world began making emergency plans to jet to California.

Local San Diego TV stations rushed to the scene and began broadcasting live, frantic updates. An all-news national cable channel, MSNBC, almost immediately broke into its programming to go live, nonstop, using footage from its local affiliate.

Suddenly—and erroneously, it turned out—the body count jumped to forty-nine. There were frenzied reports that it could go even higher.

It was then, that the San Diego County Sheriff's Department decided it had to quickly step in and substitute facts for wild speculation and rumor. A decision was made to provide frequent news conferences to spell out the basic facts.

The task fell to Commander Alan Fulmer, who was quickly surrounded by reporters, cameras, and microphones outside the mansion for a press conference, broadcast live locally and nationally.

There were a total of thirty-nine bodies, Fulmer said. All of them were men between the ages of eighteen and twenty-four. The bodies were scattered all over the house. There were no signs of a struggle, no indications of foul play. Everybody was wearing dark clothing and the upper halves of their bodies were covered by sheets.

The men were found lying on mattresses or cots with their hands at their sides as if they had fallen asleep.

There were no signs of blood and no suicide notes found—but this *was* a mass suicide, no question. And one that was well planned and well thought out.

"Our initial reaction is that it was a suicide, but we are not ruling anything out," Fulmer said. "They are all in a prone position, on their backs."

There were no children among the dead and no survivors.

"We have no idea of their identities or where they come from," Fulmer said. "We don't know if they belonged to any religious cult or group or anything like that."

It didn't matter. Hours later, headlines worthy of announcing World War III roared across the front pages of every newspaper in the world and every television and radio broadcast led with the sensational, shocking, and undeniably fascinating tale of the mass suicide in Southern California.

"39 DEAD IN CULT SUICIDE—BLOOD-
LESS HORROR IN MILLION DOLLAR
CALIFORNIA MANSION" roared the front
page of the *New York Post*, which like other
news organizations, compared the tragedy
to November 1978's mass suicide of 913 at
the People's Temple compound in the jungles of Guyana.

The story instantly became *the* topic of
conversation—trampling everything else,
even the never-ending fascination with
O.J. Simpson.

Still, San Diego law enforcement had
tossed them a disappointing press conference, reporters agreed, because thirty-nine
men don't just get together and decide to
buy the farm en masse.

What gave? And why didn't the cops
have any more knowledge about who
these thirty-nine people were, the press
demanded.

Authorities reminded reporters that this
was just a preliminary visual inspection of
the scene. They coyly added to a few journalists: stick around, there'll be more.

And there was—in spades.

Once the San Diego medical examiner

entered the picture, and the bodies and house were thoroughly examined, some amazing answers began to emerge. And less than twenty-four hours later, San Diego authorities would hold a full-scale press conference, not only to retract some of the things they had been saying, but also to add some disturbing new information that would put an incredible spin on the stunning death scene.

As the minutes grew closer to the press briefing, investigators struggled to string together a semi-complete picture. And they furiously worked to identify the leader of the group and find out if he or she were still alive. And of paramount importance, whether there were other cultists who might possibly be planning a similar suicide horror.

On Thursday afternoon, March 27, the conference room at the San Diego County Sheriff's Department contained the largest crowd of journalists in the law enforcement agency's history.

San Diego County Sheriff Bill Kolender and San Diego Medical Examiner Brian Blackbourne took the podium. In overly

sober tones, the two men methodically
weaved an incredible tale that encom-
passed religion, science fiction, computer
technology, drugs, sex, and ultimately,
madness.

As if this wasn't enough, they announced
they would show an explicit and disturbing
police videotape filmed inside the death
house. But first, they wanted to give the
facts as they knew them.

Kolender said that upon closer examination of the thirty-nine victims, the an-
nouncement that they all had been men
was in error. In fact, it was later revealed,
there were twenty women and nineteen
men in the group ranging in age from
twenty-six to seventy-two. Investigators
had at first thought all were of the same
sex because they each had extremely short
hair, shaved almost to the skin. Each was
dressed identically in baggy asexual clothing which hid all hints of male genitalia
and female breasts.

Blackbourne described how the group
had committed mass suicide and the first
thing that was apparent was that the act
had been intricately planned and carried

out as carefully as a banquet or a birthday party might have been.

The actual mechanism of death was diabolical—and flawless.

The cultists had taken their lives in three stages, with small groups helping others administer large, lethal doses of Phenobarbital and alcohol.

Phenobarbital is a powerful prescription drug used for seizure disorders with strong sedative properties that take effect in about an hour if a regular dosage is used.

An overdose triggers labored breathing and lower body temperatures which fill the lungs with fluid until a coma is induced. Alcohol accelerates the drug's actions tenfold.

That double blow would probably have been enough to finish off anybody. But the cultists wanted to make sure nothing would go wrong. So they further intensified the effects of the drugs and booze by pulling plastic bags over their heads secured by rubber bands to restrict breathing. Suffocation with a devil's mix of vodka and pills—it was a surefire way to die.

After one group succumbed to the instruments of death, the next group would clean up after them, removing the bags and making sure the body was in a dignified position and carefully covered.

In the pockets of some of the members were small handwritten notes which told of how to mix up the lethal potion; Take a small container of pudding or applesauce, mix in a large dose of crushed phenobarbitol tablets, and then wash the mixture down with straight 100 proof Vodka in several substantial gulps.

Blackbourne said the victims committed suicide beginning on March 24 with fifteen members killing themselves. The next day fifteen more took their own lives. On Wednesday, March 26, the final nine consumed the toxic dessert of pudding or applesauce, pills, and vodka.

The last two cult members alive removed the plastic bags from the heads of the last seven bodies then killed themselves. Most of the thirty-nine had identification in their pockets, Blackbourne noted.

At the moment, the medical examiner

noted, the identities would be withheld until families and next of kin were all contacted. But he said the victims represented a cross section of races including blacks, whites, and Hispanics.

They came from: New Mexico, Texas, California, Colorado, Utah, Florida, Ohio, Minnesota, Washington, Missouri, Arizona, Massachusetts, Iowa, New York, Wisconsin, Idaho, Nebraska, and Canada.

Oddly, but just as odd as anything in the case, each of the thirty-nine had a five dollar bill in his or her pocket and several quarters.

As notifications were being made, authorities said, it was apparent that many of the victims had alienated themselves from their families because of their participation in Heaven's Gate.

"Many families had not seen them in many years. For some it was a total shock," San Diego County spokesman Jack Merker told reporters.

Sheriff Kolender then addressed the question of why.

Discs in the twelve or so desktop computers on tables and desks around the house revealed that the thirty-nine victims were members of a cult called Heaven's Gate.

On a detailed World Wide Web site created by the Heaven's Gate cultists, investigators got their first indication of a motive: the followers had committed mass suicide to free themselves of their human bodies and set off to rendezvous with a UFO in outer space.

That flying saucer, they believed, was traveling closely behind the famous Hale-Bopp comet that had thrilled hundreds of millions of spectators around the world with its bright, sparkling tail.

Kolender told how the cultists decided on their ultimate act because they feared that civilization on Earth was about to end.

It was time to exit their bodies and board "a spacecraft from the Next Level"— a feat that would help them enter a higher life form.

The website hailed the Hale-Bopp comet as the herald of a spacecraft coming to "take us home to 'Their World'—in the literal 'Heavens.' "

"We are happily prepared to leave 'this

world' and go with Ti's crew," the cryptic message said on the website titled "Heaven's Gate—How and When It May Be Entered."

Just who "Ti" was, was not immediately explained.

The site also featured numerous pictures of comets, stars and other astronomical phenomena—as well as a spinning flying saucer resembling a spaceship out of a *Star Trek* episode.

"Red Alert . . . HALE-BOPP Brings Closure!" announced the site's opening words.

"Whether Hale-Bopp has a 'companion' or not is irrelevant from our perspective. However, its arrival is joyously very significant to us at Heaven's Gate.

"The joy is that our Older Member in the Evolutionary Level Above Human (the 'Kingdom of Heaven') has made it clear to us that Hale-Bopp's approach is the 'marker' we've been waiting for—the time for the arrival of the spacecraft from the Level Above Human to take us home to 'Their World'—in the literal Heavens.

"Our twenty-two years of classroom

here on Planet Earth is finally coming to
conclusion—'graduation' from the Human
Evolutionary Level.

"If you study the material on this website
you will hopefully understand our joy and
what our purpose here on Earth has been.
You may even find your 'boarding pass' to
leave with us during this brief 'window.'"

By committing mass suicide, the followers
were simply shedding their "containers" to
facilitate their journey into space.

"This was a group decision," Blackbourne
said. "Very planned, sort of immaculately
carried out."

The medical examiner and sheriff then
focused on who appeared to be behind the
nation's most bizarre tragedy in years.

His name: Marshall Herff Applewhite.

Heaven's Gate had been founded in the
Midwest some twenty or so years ago by
Applewhite, a onetime music teacher, and
his late wife, Bonnie Lu Trusdale Nettles.
Both were known to their followers by the
nursery rhyme names of "Bo" and "Peep"
as well as "Do" and "Ti"—the latter name
providing an explanation for "Ti's crew,"
the phrase on the web.

Applewhite and his followers had sent out "farewell" videos—those which had been sent to Rio D'Angelo via Federal Express—to tip the world off to their flight to another planet, the lawmen said.

The bald, wrinkled leader also encouraged his followers and others to "follow" him to another world—a better place than Earth.

Other notes around the house explained he group believed that to be able to prepare for their great exit they must faithfully abstain from all vices—drugs, alcohol, and, especially, sex.

Authorities also pointed out that they did not believe that the mass suicide of the Heaven's Gate cultists had any tie with a strange tragedy in Quebec on March 22.

On that day, five members of a doomsday cult calling itself the "Solar Temple" died in a blazing house in an apparent ritual suicide pact.

Officials noted that the inferno was part of an ongoing death wish by the group since, in both 1994 and 1995, sixty-nine members of the Solar Temple cult had died in fires in Canada and Switzerland.

They also noted that the notion that

Heaven's Gate followers had of beaming onto a spaceship that was tailing the Hale-Bopp comet was wrong.

Yes, scientists had noticed a small, bright "blip" behind Hale-Bopp. But further study revealed that the UFO was actually a dim star. It showed the further futility of the group's final flight into oblivion, the officials noted.

Reporters fired away questions like tail-gunners on a vital mission, and the sheriff and medical examiner knew they couldn't answer many of them.

So in a stroke of press relations genius, they saved the best for last. It was a three-minute videotape shot by investigators inside the house. Nothing had been touched, everything was as it was when they arrived, Blackbourne insisted.

Kolender, as if in acknowledgment of the new TV-ratings system and its concern over violence and gore, announced matter-of-factly that there would be nothing objectionable in the videotape. No blood, no gore, no guts, nothing that would dispatch a visual punch to the gut.

But when the lights were lowered and

the VCR switched on, an audience of home viewers around the world were suddenly bombarded with some of the most disturbing pictures ever broadcast on television.

Several networks showed it live.

For the first ten to twelve seconds, the video was jumpy. Then it cleared up, revealing the first body, or at least the legs. The camera then panned the legs which revealed the victim was wearing brand-new, unscuffed Nike brand sneakers. The leather and rubber appeared so shiny and bright, it seemed as though they had never been worn.

Adding to the eeriness of the scene was a video spotlight illuminating the scene, giving it a surreal quality and at the same time making it come off like a video of a raid from the show *Cops* or a poorly lit porn film.

Then another room and more bodies—four of them. They were laid out with chilling simplicity—face up on metal bunk beds, their hands at their sides. All were dressed exactly the same: in long black pants, black socks, and Nikes.

Each was covered by a triangular purple

sheet, from their thighs to the top of their shaved heads. The bodies lay on white or yellow cotton comforters and one appeared to be tucked into a green and blue plaid blanket.

In a bone-shivering touch, those who had worn eyeglasses had folded them neatly and placed them at the right side of their heads.

Each had a small overnight bag packed with clothes sitting by their feet. They appeared to be napping.

None appeared to have suffered any discomfort with their arms and legs peacefully stretched out. None had any visible jewelry or tattoos.

Their bunk beds and Army cots were neatly made with fresh linens covered by dark blankets which were soiled only by the internal juices that had dripped from the bodies.

Occasionally the video picture jiggled and shook, as if the cameraman was jolted by what he was recording.

The five rooms shown on the tape looked like college dorms inhabited by straight-A students—all neat with uncluttered desks and desk-top computers and printers.

All the garbage pails were emptied and there were no signs of any last-minute disruptions or indecision. It all looked wrong—everything was too clean, too antiseptic.

The walls had no posters, photos, or pin-ups, but were tastefully decorated with wallpaper and wooden trimming. Two sewing machines were visible in one room—each containing colored thread, as if they had been used recently to repair clothing.

The most personal touches seen were a box of tissues and a vase of flowers. An abandoned wheelchair sat beside one bed.

Detectives can be seen—clearly looking uncomfortable—as they sift through the unsettling scene.

In the videotape, the detectives are wearing white paper masks to hide the foul stench of the rotting corpses which police believe had been there for up to thirty-nine hours before being discovered. One of them points a finger at the sneakered sole of one of the victims and then nudges it slightly, as if to say, "Come on, buddy, get up, joke's over."

Large black flies could be seen buzzing throughout the rooms, apparently attracted to the decomposing corpses. The hands on two of the corpses were visible. One had small dark blotches on it—a sign that death occurred many hours earlier.

Journalists can be an offensive and irreverent lot, joking about the most horrible of things. They use black humor as a defense mechanism against the true horror of what they are really reporting about. It's an old trick and it works well. But the conference room at the San Diego County Sheriff's Department—crammed with several hundred journalists—was strangely silent. Writers and photographers stood mesmerized—stunned by the short videotape.

One reporter said the tape had reminded him of a '50s science-fiction movie that had given him nightmares as a kid. The film was *Invasion of the Body Snatchers*, in which lifeless bodies called "pods" are sent down from outer space to destroy and replace real human beings in a quest to take over Earth.

Those strangely prone bodies sure looked like pods, the reporter joked with a nervous laugh.

When the lights went back up, there was an awkward silence before a buzz began again and reporters began scrambling to make their deadlines.

Newspaper headlines screamed:

"FOLLOW ME!"

"UFO WACKOS BLASTED OFF WITH
    VODKA AND PILLS"

"COME DIE WITH ME"

"RITUAL OF DEATH!"

"UFO FREAKS LED BY 'BO' AND
    'PEEP' "

Meanwhile, as part of their prescribed therapy from a police doctor, Deputies Robert Brunk and Laura Gacek met the press to describe their feelings since witnessing the hellish scenes of death.

Discussing their thoughts, verbalizing the horrors, they explained, was the best way of exorcising the demons.

"The gamut of emotions I've experienced in the last few days is very hard to describe. It's nothing I would wish on anyone," Brunk said in a steady but weathered voice.

Gacek was just as solemn. "It was one of the most bizarre things you would ever hope to see," she said.

Police also unveiled pictures they had taken of some artwork in the house. One drawing was of a dome-headed alien with large black eyes not unlike "the head of an alien you would see on *The X-Files*," one official remarked.

Dr. Blackbourne and his staff had been burning the candle at both ends for three days to finish autopsies on the thirty-nine victims. It had been tough going from the moment the bodies were removed from the house. One of the morgue workers transporting the corpses almost passed out because even though they were in thick plastic body bags, the stench still got out.

Blackbourne's initial visual examination of the cultists did not produce anything extraordinary. Except for the advancing state of decomposition, none of the bodies had any distinguishing marks, bruises, or scars.

A closer inspection revealed otherwise.

And as Blackbourne approached the podium in the conference room at the San Diego County Sheriff's Department on March 28, he knew that what he was about to say was going to be like throwing a side of raw beef into a den of hungry lions.

The fact was that Applewhite and five of his male followers had been surgically castrated.

The room exploded—with radio reporters and producers with cell phones jabbering furiously to their desks. "Jesus Christ—the guy had his balls hacked off!" one scribe yelled with the glee of somebody who had just discovered the Holy Grail.

"But these scars don't appear recent," Blackbourne continued. "They were done quite some time ago. Quite strange, I'd say. Quite strange."

"SECT HAD EUNUCH APPROACH TO FAITH", screamed the *New York Post* the next day.

"FROM PURPLE SHROUDS TO SPACE SHIPS TO CASTRATION", the *New York Times* shouted.

The question now was why. Why did six members of Heaven's Gate have their testicles removed. Authorities theorized that because the cult had a policy of no sex, the lack of testicles would surely curb the male sexual appetite.

Yes. But to go to such an extreme. Of course, voluntary castration was certainly not unheard of. In the sixteenth and seventeenth centuries, it was common for rabidly devout priests to cut their testicles off as a sign of absolute devotion to God. With their sex drive gone, it would be much easier to avoid the temptations of the flesh.

But voluntary castration today? There was something behind this. Something fishy. And investigators were on a hunt to find it.

As the testicle mystery loomed, Blackbourne also revealed that toxicology tests had come back showing that many of the victims had swallowed three times the lethal dosage of phenobarbital in their systems. Others died of suffocation.

Detectives announced they were opening up a new area of their investigation: Exactly how did the group manage to acquire such massive amounts of phenobarbital to kill themselves.

They said that a lethal dose amounted to fifty tablets for each person. "We're talking probably more than a thousand tablets here," one investigator said.

Four days after the mass suicide was discovered, the press published a complete list of the victims. And instantly, the hunt was on for families, friends, and acquaintances of the dead as journalists tried to uncover what had led them to such a drastic finality.

Aside from Applewhite, the victims were:

1. Dana Tracey Abreo, 35,
   of Denver, Colorado.
2. Marshall Herff Applewhite, 65.
3. Robert John Arancio, 46,
   of Dallas, Texas.
4. Raymond Alan Bowers, 45,
   of Jupiter, Florida.
5. LaDonna Ann Brugato, 40,
   of Englewood, Colorado.
6. Margaret June Bull, 53,
   of Ellensburg, Washington.
7. Cheryl Elaine Butcher, 43,
   of Springfield, Missouri.
8. Michael Howard Carrier, 48.
9. Suzanne Sylvia Cooke, 54.
10. John M. Craig, 63,
    of Durango, Colorado.

11. Betty Deal, 64.
12. Erika Ernst, 40,
    of Calgary, Canada.
13. Alphonso Ricardo Foster, 44,
    of Detroit, Michigan.
14. Lawrence Jackson Gale, 47,
    of Lake Forest, California.
15. Darwin Lee Johnson, 42,
    of Orem, Utah.
16. Julie Lamontagne, 45,
    of Amherst, Massachusetts.
17. Jackie Leonard, 72,
    of Littleton, Colorado.
18. Jeffrey Howard Lewis, 41,
    of San Antonio, Texas.
19. Gail Renee Maeder, 28,
    of Sag Harbor, New York.
20. Steven Terry McCarter, 41,
    of Albuquerque, New Mexico.
21. Joel Peter McCormick, 29,
    of Madison, Wisconsin.
22. Yvonne McCurdy-Hill, 39,
    of Cincinnati, Ohio.
23. David Geoffery Moore, 41,
    of Los Gatos, California.
24. Nancy Dianne Nelson, 45,
    of Mesa, Arizona.

25. Norma Jeane Nelson, 59,
    of North Dallas, Texas.
26. Thomas Alva Nichols, 59,
    of Arizona.
27. Susan Elizabeth Nora Paup, 54.
28. Lindley Ayerhart Pease, 41,
    of New Hampshire.
29. Lucy Eva Pesho, 63,
    of New Mexico.
30. Margaret Ella Richter, 46,
    of Oroville, California.
31. Judith Ann Rowland, 50,
    of Dallas, Texas.
32. Michael Barr Sandoe, 26,
    Boulder, Colorado.
33. Brian Alan Schaaf, 40.
34. Joyce Angela Skalla, 58.
35. Gary Jordan St. Louis, 44,
    of Idaho.
36. Susan Frances Strom, 44,
    of Omaha, Nebraska.
37. Denise June Thurman, 44,
    of Locust Valley, New York.
38. David Cabot Van Sinderen, 48,
    of Connecticut.
39. Gordon Thomas Welch, 50,
    of Arizona.

None of the thirty-nine victims were famous—but there was one eerie twist to one of the victims' pasts. Thomas Nichols, it turned out, was the kid brother of TV star Nichelle Nichols, who played "Lt. Uhura" on the original *Star Trek* series.

"My brother was a highly intelligent and beautiful man. He made his choices and we respect those choices," Nichelle Nichols would say.

Oddly, as police would learn from friends of the victims, the cult regularly watched *Star Trek* on TV and had open discussions about its plots and actors.

The "Lt. Uhura" connection was incredible, but it was quickly forgotten when the riddle of the castrated cultists appeared to be solved.

The *New York Post* reported that Applewhite—Father John as his Rancho Santa Fe neighbors had known him—had been fired from his post as music professor at the University of Alabama at Tuscaloosa in the 1960s.

The reason? Administrators learned he was involved in a steamy homosexual relationship with a student.

Married with two kids, Applewhite got

another job at the University of St. Thomas in Houston. But his urges to sleep with young men returned and he was fired in a similar scandal.

Reports told how the student once described how the pair had enjoyed full intercourse in Applewhite's house while his wife slept nearby. Apparently, Applewhite was turned on by the fact he was doing something dangerous and kinky so close to his spouse.

One source who spoke to the student told the *New York Post:*

"The student talked about how frightening it was being in the next room, and how the teacher enjoyed some sort of thrill in this behavior with his wife so close."

UFO cults author James Lewis said a depressed and ashamed Applewhite checked into a psychiatric hospital the following year and asked to be "cured" of his homosexual desires.

It was there he met Bonnie Nettles, who had long talks with him about his conflicts. The two became spiritual mates and when Applewhite left the hospital, he dumped his first wife and married Nettles, who would eventually become the co-founder of Heaven's Gate. Applewhite and Nettles were on the same wavelength as far as physical desire were concerned. They would not have sex with each other it was agreed. The marriage, therefore, was never consummated.

The question now: Was Applewhite's cult, with its science-fiction mumbo jumbo about "shedding containers" and going to another world, just the offshoot of a sexually tortured man's inability to cope?

Was his lifelong lust for men—and his guilt over it—the ultimate reason for the castrations, and eventually the mass suicide?

The conclusive answer from the experts was "maybe."

"It sounds like this was someone who was guilt-ridden that he was having homosexual attractions, and he wanted to do something about it," explained Dr. Fred Berlin, founder of a sexual disorders clinic at Johns Hopkins University.

"The easiest way to do this is to lower the level of testosterone in the body—but an irreversible surgical procedure would probably be a last resort," Berlin said.

Investigators noticed that in one of the "farewell" messages, one male member referred to the joy of having his "vehicle neutered"—an apparent reference to his castration—and "how free that has made me feel."

And they also found an earlier tape made by Applewhite in which he sternly told of the cult's distaste for sexual activity of any kind.

"It is evil, because it is barbaric and it is beneath me," he proclaimed.

But would depression, obsession, and hysteria over sex really cause one to kill himself and convince many others to do the same? There were suggestions that Applewhite had other problems as well.

According to CNN and *Newsweek* magazine, members of the Heaven's Gate cult believed Marshall Applewhite was dying of cancer.

Applewhite believed he may have had only six months to live and told his followers his body was "disintegrating." An Applewhite confidant, science-fiction writer Lee Shargel, said the cult guru had told him he had liver cancer.

Could this have sparked the tragedy?

Cult members were apparently upset by Applewhite's disclosure as evidenced by a message by one female cult member found on a computer disc.

"Once he is gone there is nothing left here on the face of the Earth for me— no reason to stay a moment longer," the unidentified member had written.

But Medical Examiner Blackbourne said the preliminary autopsy results on Applewhite showed he did not suffer from terminal cancer.

"Marshall Applewhite has no gross physical evidence and no visual evidence of cancer in his liver or any other organs," Blackbourne said.

"He did have some coronary artery disease. At sixty-six, it's not unreasonable to expect he would."

Another mystery arose as it was disclosed the cult had been attempting to make a Hollywood movie in the months before their mass suicide.

They had hoped to spread their bizarre, no-sex, science-fiction views across America, according to film executives.

Alex Papas, a Phoenix, Arizona, producer

who met the cultists when they were renting a house in Arizona, said they used him in late 1995 to launch the project.

It was based on their concepts about life on Earth and how the ultimate goal was to move on to the "Kingdom of God."

Programmers at NBC had shown some interest in financing the picture, but they lost interest in it believing it was too way out.

Rick Singer, a Los Angeles TV and movie producer and Papas's partner, said he had received a telephone call from one of the cult members just two weeks ago.

"They were a little weird the way they looked and dressed, but they were so eager and so enthusiastic," Singer said.

"It would have been more likely that they would have wanted to live for a couple of hundred years just so they could keep their eyes glued to a telescope."

Papas, who runs Way Out Pictures, said that in September 1995 two cult members subleased a $450,000 home in Paradise Valley, Arizona The cultists shelled out $3,400 a month to rent the 5,400-square-foot, six-bedroom house.

A few weeks after they moved in, Papas said the group gave him a 223-page screenplay titled *Beyond Human: Return of the Next Level.*

The intricate plot featured motherships, alien abductions, and clashes between evil aliens resembling lizards and friendly aliens over control of Earth. The story told of the aliens' ability to rise up to a level several flights above humans. The script was certainly fantastic, but it didn't seem to be geared enough towards a general audience.

Disappointed, but more determined than ever, the members worked around the clock to polish and refine the rambling science-fiction teleplay in hopes of getting it on the air.

Ironically, the project had been actively discussed just two weeks before the mass suicide. It just didn't make sense to Papas.

"They were rational, lucid, reasonable people. They were easy to talk to and were real interested in getting their script out into the public," he said.

Papas said he had worked for months with group members Otis Paceman and Rio DiAngelo—the soon-to-be ex-cultist who would receive the "farewell" tapes and discover the suicides.

Papas then turned the completed script over to Singer, who said he presented it to NBC. The network decided against it.

He said he had several informal lunch meetings with cult members after the NBC rejection and then got a call two weeks ago from DiAngelo.

"He said he had left the group and he wanted to move forward with the teleplay," Singer said. "That's what we were planning to do when all this happened. They were so thankful about what I was doing. I would have given long odds that they would have wanted to do something like this."

Could it possibly be that the cultists were so disappointed in the slow progress of their script that they committed suicide to "beef up" the project. Death for art, as it were? It was one theory being looked at by authorities.

Why members would "do something like this," as producer Rick Singer had mentioned, had become the hot topic on talk radio and TV, which devoted hours and hours to hundreds of different theories and opinions.

Chapter

3

A WORLD ABUZZ

Reaction came quickly from all corners—from people who'd been inside the suicide cult, to psychiatrists, social workers, criminalists, politicians, the man on the street.

One former member whose wife was among the dead came forward to say he was sorry he'd missed the group's final act.

Wayne Cooke of Sausalito, California also said he was totally convinced that his wife, Suzanne Sylvia Cooke, had, in fact, "shed her container" and was now aboard a spaceship with her thirty-eight fellow brothers and sisters.

"I believe they are on a craft somewhere,

whether it's behind the comet or not, I really don't know," Wayne Cooke said in an interview on KQED-FM on San Francisco.

Cooke said he left the cult three years ago but still supported its beliefs of rejecting sexual activity, alcohol, and all earthly possessions in order to evolve to a higher level.

"I wish I had the strength to have remained, to have stuck it out and gotten stronger and continued to be a part of that group," he later told CBS' *60 Minutes*.

Cooke said that despite the view by some that Applewhite and his followers were severely disturbed people, what they did together should not be considered crazy.

"I'm not suicidal . . . but I have no problem in laying down my shell, or my body, as they did that day. I don't consider it suicide."

While they were trooping across the country with Applewhite, cult members believed they might someday be transformed into E.T.-type aliens on Earth and beamed up into a spacecraft for the ride to the "Level Above Humans." But it might mean suicide first, they realized.

"At first we thought we'd be taking our

bodies with us in a condition that would have changed. But before the craft came we might be required to get rid of the body. It would be a leap of faith," Cooke said.

Another former cult member who identified himself only as "Sawyer" told *60 Minutes:*

"Suicide isn't the proper term for what they did, in my opinion. They left their bodies. It was something they were preparing for for a long time. It was not a traumatic thing to them.

"In my opinion, it was like going to bed and knowing that they would wake up still alive but not in their bodies."

Preparation for the journey to the heavens was "a very difficult endeavor"—and part of that difficulty was celibacy.

Sawyer, who joined the cult with a girlfriend after attending a meeting in Oregon in the early '70s, said they never had sex again.

He knew five cult members and Applewhite were undergoing castration and "I wanted to very badly at the time."

"I flipped a coin," he said, explaining why he hadn't had his testicles cut out. Asked whether he was glad he avoided the procedure, he said, "I lost."

The two ex-cultists added chilling epilogues to their statements, saying they both believed there were scores that still remain faithful to the cult's principles and that members could be beamed into space by shedding their human bodies.

Cooke, an "off and on" member of the cult for twenty-three years, did not explain why he left but acknowledged that he and his wife abandoned their daughter Kelly to follow the cult two decades back when she was only ten.

Kelly said while she had never accepted or followed the cult's rules and regulations, she accepted her mother's death.

"My understanding was that it was to go to the next level, to be with God. I don't believe she committed suicide. That's a strong word to use when you consider that this is something she worked for all her life. She graduated to the next level," Kelly said.

Wayne Cooke disputed the term "brainwashing."

"We wanted our brains washed. There's a lot of joy in it [and] they reached a point that the word was given to depart from this world back to the mother ship," he said.

"To move into bodies that had been prepared for them, physical bodies of a finer nature—androgynous, sexless. It's an evolutionary step. They left when a comet came. A comet has significance, historically. They left in the Easter Week. That has significance historically.

"They left by laying down their bodies, that has enormous impact. Obviously a stage is being set by the next level for this world, for others, to examine this."

Cooke exploded one mystery that had police puzzled—the question of the five dollar bill and several quarters tucked neatly inside each victim's slacks.

"Whenever we went to a movie or went out for any reason we always took five dollars and change, in case we suddenly needed to use the telephone, we had a quarter or two in our pocket," Cooke said.

"We would have five dollars if the car broke down and for some reason we needed a taxi," Cooke said.

He went on to describe the cult's "procedures" for tasks ranging from going to the bathroom to washing cars. "In showering, because we often shared the same house, we would often not use any more water than necessary, so we would scrub down and then rinse off.

"They were practical, to-the-point guidelines that had to do with living within the budget of your supplies. Let's say you might have so many supplies on board your craft to go from one star system to another, so they you would always live within that budget," he said.

Law enforcement authorities had put out the word—anybody with any information about what happened should call them. And many people did—although some offered theories that were out of this world.

Several callers suggested that just like the full moon is rumored to make people act wild and crazy, the appearance of a comet can do the same, except with increased intensity.

Throughout history, comets have been considered signs of good fortune—and also of doom.

▽   ▽   ▽

"Initially comets were thought to be an atmospheric phenomenon. Then in the Middle Ages comets were thought to be warning shots fired at a sinful Earth from the right hand of a vengeful God," explained Donald Yeomans of the Jet Propulsion Laboratory in Pasadena, California.

Yeomans, author of *Comets: a Chronological History of Observation, Science, Myth and Folklore,* said such links between comets and death have dominated history.

One early mention of a memorable comet streak occurred in 44 B.C., when the Roman Emperor Augustus dedicated a temple to a large comet visible during athletic games in that year—just after the bloody assassination of Julius Caesar.

"The common people assumed that it was the soul of Caesar on its way to the region of the immortal gods," Yeomans said. Augustus used a comet on some coins struck during his rule, "perhaps to remind his subjects that the reins of power had passed to him from the hands of his now deified father."

As science studied comets, "there was gradual transformation of comets as warnings to agents of destruction," Yeomans said.

In 1773, Parisians were sent into a panicked frenzy after Joseph-Jerome Lefrancais de Lalande revealed a paper on his computations that sixty-one comets had orbits that brought them close to Earth. While he had written that any chance of a collision was slim, he had neglected to emphasize the point.

The great comet of 1843 saw another panic advanced by William Miller and his followers, the Millerites. The comet was seen as a starry signal confirming Miller's belief the Earth would be wiped out in a hellish inferno. But the Earth did not end as Miller predicted on April 3 of that year.

University of Maryland astronomer Lucy McFadden said it was shocking to think in the age of the computer that groups like Heaven's Gate were relying on rumors and myths.

"It's ironic in the day of the World Wide Web, when there's so much information available, that there are people who choose to have their beliefs take them so far from the truth," she said.

As the awe-inspiring Hale-Bopp comet made its way across the skies in a spectacu-

lar cosmic light show, this might have been
the signal Heaven's Gate members had
waited for, astronomers told authorities.

And Hale-Bopp certainly had clout, a lot
more clout than many other comets, there
was no doubt of that. One of the largest
comets ever cataloged by scientists, Hale-
Bopp had a tail estimated at ten million to
twenty million miles in length and a nucleus
of twenty miles to thirty miles across. It was
also roughly three to four times bigger than
Halley's comet. And it was believed that
Hale-Bopp had not visited the Earth's territory for about 4,000 years.

Like many amazing cosmic finds, it was
suddenly noticed in the middle of the night
by telescope as it was about 100 million
miles away on July 23, 1995 by Alan Hale
of the Southwest Institute for Space
Research in Cloudcroft, New Mexico, and
Thomas Bopp, an amateur astronomer from
Glendale, Arizona.

Hale was distressed that the beautiful
comet bearing his name had somehow
inspired people to kill themselves, but said
the concept was nothing new.

"There have been people all along who

have been attaching apocalyptic significance to Hale-Bopp. Clearly, there seem to
have been at least thirty-nine people who
believed something," Hale said.

Police technicians who specialize in computer investigations searched for answers in
a website created by the Heaven's Gate
cultists called "Higher Source." The site is an
advertisement for computer services some
of the cultists proficient in computer technology offered in order to make money and
finance their group.

The site revealed a highly sophisticated,
business-oriented endeavor, police—and
anybody who clicked onto the web—found
out.

The website, while it did not contain any
overtly religious material—featured back-
grounds of stars and spectacular galactic
imagery. On their Higher Source site, the
group's computer whizzes boasted of running a sophisticated website design company
as well as offering programming, systems
analysis, and computer security services.

"We at Higher Source not only cater to

customizing websites that will enhance your company image, but strive to make your transition into the 'world of cyberspace' a very easy and fascinating experience," the site said.

It also listed numerous websites that Higher Source had designed, mostly for businesses located in the San Diego area including the prestigious San Diego Polo Club, a parts supplier for British cars, and a film production company.

Strangely, one of the film company's upcoming features is coincidentally titled, *The Last Time I Committed Suicide*.

Heather Chronert, officer manager of the San Diego Polo Club, said the cultists had been buzzing about Hale-Bopp.

"I said, 'What's the Hale-Bopp?' They looked at me like I was crazy and said it's a great comet coming in March and April," she told *Newsday*, a Long Island newspaper.

Aside from their enthusiasm about the comet, the designers and technical writers who worked with Chronert rarely discussed their beliefs or personal lives.

Once, one of the women mentioned to Chronert that she had always been a "nerd." Now the woman felt happy being a "computer nerd," Chronert said.

"They were odd because they dressed differently, but they were really nice," she told *Newsday*. "They wore colorless shirts, billowy kind of pants, and sometimes they came in with jogging suits on. They always wore tennis shoes, and they all had very short haircuts. Some were even bald."

Two or three weeks ago Chronert received a call from one of the workers. "They said they would be busy with monastery activities until after Easter," she said. "If I had any problems I would have to wait until then."

One of the last projects the company appears to have been working on was an online magazine for young people that focused on horse racing. When Howard Bass, manager of media services for Thoroughbred Racing Communications,. returned to his New York City office at the end of February there was a message from a woman named June Maguiar at Higher Source.

"She said they were doing a web page for a company that produces handicapping

software, which helps you pick winners,"
said Bass, who publishes a weekly newslet-
ter about thoroughbred horses.

"This company wanted to set up a page
that had more than just gambling on it.
They needed editorial content. So they
called us and asked to receive our weekly e-
mail."

Bass suggested she call John Lee, manager
of broadcast services with the New York
Racing Association. "She said, 'We're a religious community, and we make our living by
designing web pages and working on software,'" said Lee.

"She sent me more detailed information
about the project and more about the company, Higher Source," said Lee, who sent
her some racing information. "I remember
I did look up their web pages and their earlier clients and saw a few looked to be
rather New Agey but others were more
corporate."

The site notes "The Difference" of the
Higher Source group.

"The individuals at the core of our group
have worked closely together for over
twenty years. During those years, each of us

has developed a high degree of skill and know-how through personal discipline and concerted effort," it said.

"We try to stay positive in every circumstance and put the good of a project above any personal concerns or artistic egos. By sustaining this attitude and conduct, we have achieved a high level of efficiency and quality in our work. This crew-minded effort, combined with ingenuity and creativity, have helped us provide advanced solutions at highly competitive rates."

Strangely optimistic words for a group planning such a monumental act, investigators thought.

Meanwhile, residents of Rancho Santa Fe tried to come to grips with the horrifying tragedy in their community, the "Beverly Hills of San Diego."

On Easter Sunday at the crack of dawn, three hundred worshipers gathered by the death house and praised God as the sole keeper of heaven's gate.

"Jesus Christ is the gate, he's the only way. There's no UFO waiting behind a comet," Pastor Bob Botsford told the non-denominational flock, who wore Easter hats and flowers on their lapels and dresses. His read a sermon titled "The Key to Heaven's Gate." In it, he warned that the entrance to heaven was quite narrow and "only one person can pass through at a time. You can't get in because you belong to some group."

The worshippers vigorously nodded their heads in approval.

"God created us. He didn't create us to take our lives," one woman said as she shivered in the early morning chill.

Applewhite's sixty-nine-year-old sister Louise Winant didn't know about that or anything about her brother's alleged sexual weirdness. She only wanted to remember the nice things.

"He was a very loving, caring person. Very intelligent and had a wonderful singing voice," Winant said.

"Oh, he sang beautifully. He could play almost anything. He was extremely talented."

Sheriff Bill Kolender acknowledged Applewhite's talent for getting people to follow his word, regardless of how sick and twisted it was. Kolender is still searching for answers, answers that will forever go unsolved.

"Who or what would make thirty-nine people take their life in this manner?" Kolender asked. "I told myself that the question cannot be answered in terms, I think, that the rest of us will ever understand."

Chapter

4

BO, PEEP, AND
THE TRAVELING UFO SHOW

The seeds of doom were planted twenty-seven years ago, when a sexually confused, failed singer-turned-music-teacher met a dreamy, strong-willed nurse four years his senior.

"I felt I had known her forever," Marshall Applewhite told a *New York Times Magazine* writer about Bonnie Lu Nettles in 1976. "I had wanted someone to do an astrological chart on me, so when I met her, I ran right to my car and got my birth certificate."

They had not only found each other—but a common, deluded history and a shared, doomed destiny.

In 1970, Marshall Herff Applewhite was a strikingly handsome thirty-eight-year-old musician who looked back with disappointment at the dream that never came true—the life of a professional singer in New York City—and with bitterness at a sexual orientation that disgusted him.

Bonnie was a plain-speaking, dowdy-looking mother of four who was a nurse with an avocation for astrology and the occult, and an unshakable belief in reincarnation.

They decided at once they had known each other in previous lives.

Applewhite and Nettles met in 1970. Just where and how depends on who's talking.

According to his family, Applewhite suffered heart problems that landed him in a Houston hospital. Others knew a darker secret: Applewhite was fast losing his mind, hearing voices, and battling with the demons of his confused sexuality—and Nettles was the angel in white who rescued him.

According to the *Washington Post*, Applewhite checked into a psychiatric hospital to be "cured" of his homosexual desires.

So guilty did the gifted music teacher feel

about his homosexual affairs, that he "confided to at least one of his lovers his longing for a meaningful, platonic relationship where he could develop his full potential without sexual entanglements," University of Montana sociologist Robert Balch told the *Washington Post*.

For sure, there was no sexual energy generated between Applewhite and Nettles. But there was a compulsive attraction "to discover what had brought them together," Applewhite would write years later.

At some point in the '70s, Applewhite had himself castrated.

"Applewhite was so alienated from his homosexuality that he was teaching people not to have sex," said James Lewis of the Institute for the Study of American Religion who has studied Applewhite and Nettles's group for more than twenty years. "He would put people of opposite sexes together and force them to learn to become neutral, nonsexual."

In his monotonous and self-important ramblings about his spiritual journey that spilled onto the Internet in the 1990s, Applewhite provided a sketchy account of his life twenty years beforehand. It was uncharacteristically succinct, free of cult babble, and self-effacing.

Writing under his cult moniker "Do," Applewhite described himself as "a divorcee who had lived with a male friend for some years, (and) was contentedly involved in cultural and academic activities."

Just as Appelwhite was wrestling with his sexuality in the '70s—a secret he fastidiously hid from his family and friends from his pre-cult life—science's view of homosexuality was evolving rapidly. Some psychologists in the '70s still believed it possible to "cure" homosexuality.

There was no way Applewhite, son of a preacher, was going to come running out of the closet in 1970—to his family at least. So embarrassed by the raging internal battle he was fighting, and perhaps sensitive to the mores of a different generation, Applewhite simply lied when he told his sister about a needed hospitalization.

All Louise Winant of Port Aransas, Texas, knew was that her brother had a heart problem, a "heart block," and needed to be hospitalized.

Winant described her brother's illness as a "near-death experience." The cure seemed to frighten Applewhite's family far more than the disease.

"He had an illness in Houston and one of the nurses there told him that he had a purpose, that God kept him alive," Winant said. "She sort of talked him into the fact that this was the purpose—to lead these people—and he took it from there."

In Nettles, Applewhite found "the platonic helper he had longed for all his life," Balch told the *Washington Post.*

The odd-looking couple—one lean and handsome, the other dowdy and plain, became inseparable. But the importance of their alliance went way beyond their ying-yang affinity. Their first meeting would have explosive consequences almost from the start.

Each would turn away from their old lives from that day forward. There was no going back, and seemingly, no desire to do so for this nondescript couple who looked like Iowans, but spoke like visitors from another planet.

They found in each other what no one had seen, or guessed, before. They fed each other's fantasies, and completed them. It took virtually no time before the pair's outlandish theories would rattle the world.

In an interview published in the *Houston Post* in 1972, Nettles brashly declared to the world that she was assisted in her astrological work by a monk named Brother Francis who had died in 1818.

"He stands beside me when I interpret the charts," she said. "There can be several meanings to them, and if I'm wrong, he will correct me."

Applewhite supported her story of getting help from a dead monk. He was already showing an uncanny knack for turning the weird into the plausible, even wonderful.

"We know that we are putting ourselves in jeopardy with three-fourths of the people of our past," he told the Houston paper. "A lot of people are going to say, 'Old applesauce finally flipped.'"

It may have been the only prediction Applewhite got right.

The day the interview appeared, Applewhite was promptly booted from his job as director of music at St. Mark's Episcopal Church in Houston.

There's no doubt that Nettles, ever the mild-mannered nurse, held considerable power over Applewhite.

It was this nurse from Texas, with her eyes on the stars, who would help incarnate Applewhite as a Jesus for the New Age. She would anoint him as the leader, and he would cling to it, nurture it, and finally turn the mission toward an incredible, hopeless end.

"We tried to talk him out of this," Applewhite's sister said. "But he said, 'You don't know me.' He was a sincere man and I'm sure he believed everything he talked about."

To the outside world, Applewhite and Nettles had developed something that combined spaced-out theology and hip evangelism.

But on closer look, their spiritual flying saucer philosophy was nothing more than a mish-mash of the themes from a couple of science-fiction books that were wildly popular at the time.

One of them was Alison Lurie's *Imaginary Friends,* published in 1967, which told of the "Truth Seekers," a devoted group living in a small American city.

They believed they made contact with superior beings who have long since transcended material bodies and populate a planet called Varna, light years away from Earth.

The book also describes how scouts from Varna observe the solar system from their spaceship and through "cosmic vibrations." The Varnians then guide the Truth Seekers' spiritual development toward "higher planes."

A second popular science-fiction thriller, Robert A. Heinlein's *Stranger in a Strange Land*, first published in 1961, tells the story of a superhuman being from Mars who comes to earth with a highly idealistic message, wins converts, incurs the wrath of the locals, and is stoned and beaten to death. In his superhuman state, the creature returns to Mars with some of his followers to pursue new assignments.

New Age messiahs Applewhite and Nettles constantly gave themselves different names, Bo and Peep—or sometimes Tiddly and Wink, or even Winnie and Pooh—and concocted a blend of astral blather and spiritual revivalism.

They were convinced they had both been dropped on Earth from outer space, and would go back there on the next available flying saucer. They intended to take passengers, recruiting lost souls with little to lose on Earth who hoped to gain everything in a starry, pain-free outer space.

"There are a lot of spacecraft up there," in the heavens, Bo told his *New York Times Magazine* interviewer in 1976. "It is a misguided religious concept that members in the real heaven do not use transportation. The spacecraft are a means for getting from one place to another."

Neither of these New Age messiahs cared how the message played to the little old lady in Iowa—or even with their wives, husbands, and kids who became little more than excess baggage.

Applewhite had two children he last saw in the early 1970s. Today one of them, Mark Applewhite, forty, lives in Corpus Christi, and works at the Annapolis Christian Church. He has two children of his own.

The younger Applewhite said he last saw his father when he was five and his parents were getting divorced. He said he knew little about the cult and hadn't heard from his father in more than twenty-five years.

"I am appalled by the things that have resulted from the actions of my father and others in that cult," Applewhite said in a statement.

He told the Associated Press that he, his wife and two children are Christians "with the real ticket to heaven."

He also said he has a thirty-six-year-old sister, and that his mother is still alive. But he will not say where.

"It's not ever easy, but when you believe in the Lord Jesus Christ, it's easier to forgive," he said.

Neither Applewhite nor Nettles ever cared much about forgiveness from those who were attached to their old lives.

Without their former jobs and families, Bo and Peep opened a nondescript little storefront in Houston and dubbed it the Christian Arts Center, hawking astrology, mysticism, healing, metaphysics, theosophy and comparative religions.

It was a spectacular failure.

"It was just an excuse for our awakening," Nettles told the *New York Times Magazine.* "A means for us to understand what we were about."

Translated: Bo and Peep were preparing their act for the road. It would take a year to pull it all together, this talk of "higher levels" and flying saucers.

"Our thirst was unquenched and we were not finding what our purpose was," Bo would say. "It was as if the season had arrived under the direction of the next level for us to awaken to what we had to do.

"It was as if we had been given smelling salts and told, 'O.K. you guys. You've had forty years and now it's time for you to realize who you are, what you have to do and get on with the show.'"

Their transformation—they would later refer to the shedding of their old lives as "The Process" and they demanded no less of their followers—was profound beyond belief.

Bo and Peep decided they were not just reincarnated, but had existed before in the heavens itself, in the "level above human."

Their astral attachment was a stunning detour from a road that had been nothing if not unremarkable, even mundane.

Born in Spur, Texas, Applewhite attended Austin College, a Presbyterian-affiliated institution in Sherman, Texas, then studied music at the University of Colorado.

After he married his wife, Ann, the couple moved to New York, where he hoped to become a professional singer. He also sang and studied music in Germany, according to his biography in a 1966 Houston Grand Opera program.

But the Big Apple, the theater capital of the world, was where Applewhite pegged his dreams of making it as a professional singer.

"He didn't get the roles," retired professor Charles Byers of Mesa, Arizona, told the *Denver Post*. "He was doing a lot of commercials, making a living."

In 1952, he enrolled at the Presbyterian seminary in Richmond, Virginia, where he spent one year. Hal Todd, vice president of the seminary, told the *Washington Post* that Applewhite's year there appeared to be unremarkable.

Applewhite was recruited in 1953 by the minister of the First Presbyterian Church in Gastonia, North Carolina, to become the

choir director, said Edith Warren, a member
of the church, to the *Washington Post.* Warren,
who described herself as a close friend of
Applewhite and his wife, called the future
cult leader "very personable, very intelligent.

"He and his wife, I just enjoyed being
with them," Warren commented from her
home in Gastonia. Warren said Applewhite
and his wife lived in a rented apartment
during the two years they were in
Gastonia. She said the couple gave birth to
a boy while they lived in the town. "He
was quite a musician and had a beautiful
voice," she told the *Washington Post.*

Those who knew Applewhite at Colorado
recalled him similarly.

"He did a lot of work with musicals,"
Byers told the *Denver Post.* "He was happy-
go-lucky, popular with students."

Applewhite played the lead in "South
Pacific" and "Oklahoma" at the university,
Byers said.

By 1961, Applewhite was hired by the
University of Alabama, where one former
student claimed dramatic personal changes
were taking place.

"When I first met him, he was Mr.

Straight-Laced, married, with a couple of kids," said David Daniel, who said he took voice lessons from Applewhite.

It was during his time at the University of Alabama where Applewhite's sexual preferences turned to men.

"During that year, he sort of went crazy, became gay," Daniel claimed.

"He seemed so straight in Tuscaloosa, and the next thing you know he's sleeping with one of his students, a man."

Daniel said Applewhite left the University "in enormous disgrace.

"He became so flighty and socialized with and drank with students. He so blatantly ignored his own faculty. He had a very visible relationship with one male student," Daniel said.

Applewhite was hard to resist—"devastatingly handsome," according to those who knew him.

"He was Mr. All-America: big smile, very tan, very well built," Daniel said. "His eyes were blue, the bluest eyes I've ever seen. And the whitest, biggest teeth. The kids called him Mr. Ipana because that was a toothpaste at the time."

A spokesman for the University of Alabama in Tuscaloosa insisted Applewhite "resigned in good standing," but there were many others besides Daniel who knew Applewhite at the university, and who say he openly flaunted the scandalous relationship that cost him his job.

According to university records, Applewhite was hired in May 1961 as an associate professor to teach a choral group and voice instruction, and submitted his letter of resignation in 1964. Those who knew him paint a dark portrait of the teacher's time at the school.

There were others who corroborated the accounts of Applewhite's homosexuality. One said the head of the music department at the time, Dr. Wilbur Rowand, was furious when he found out about Applewhite's affair with a student, and immediately fired Applewhite, who then went by his middle name, Herff.

"The chairman was a very tough, stern man and when he found out about it, he fired Herff in a second. That was it, he was gone," the *New York Post* quoted one unnamed faculty person.

The chairman's widow, Harriet Rowand,

said she had heard stories of Applewhite's unethical and bizarre behavior but said that she only knew them as rumors, adding that her husband never spoke about him.

"He was a very nice young man who did a good job, but I don't know the reason my husband fired him. It was around that time that he left his wife and children," Rowand said.

Rowand said the FBI interviewed her husband at least three times in the late '60s and early '70s about the disgraced teacher's newly acquired interest in cult activity—long after Applewhite had left, his marriage in tatters, his future in doubt, his present a scandal.

The *New York Post* also reported that a former University of Alabama student once described how the pair had sex in the teacher's house while his wife slept in the adjoining room.

"The student talked about how frightening it was being in the next room, and how the teacher enjoyed some sort of thrill in this behavior with his wife so close."

Amanda Penick, a piano teacher at the school when Applewhite taught there, said she saw him change from a gifted, ruggedly handsome teacher to a man whose behavior turned incredibly erratic during his three-year stay at the university.

"He was quite wonderful before all the strangeness," Penick said. "Even after all this time, I could never forget about a person like that."

Equally unforgettable was a bizarre dinner party, she recalled.

"I went to a dinner party with him and his wife and my husband and he behaved extremely peculiarly," Penick said. "He in fact disappeared after we first got there, left his wife, and said he was comforting a fellow parishioner. He reappeared briefly and was gone again, and then called again and said he would not be coming back.

"We were saddled with his wife for that night, and we had to take her home. I've never known anyone to do anything like that since."

Penick said she had the distinct feeling that behind the sudden disappearance was Applewhite's involvement in a hurried sexual tryst.

Once fired from the university, there seemed no place else to go for the disappointed, lonely and shamed Applewhite. He drifted back to his home state of Texas.

His marriage, too, was busting up.

But the music was still inside him, the talent fairly in tact. There would be life again, it seemed for the energetic Applewhite, despite the losses, despite the disappointments. Everyone around him in Texas believed it perhaps more than he.

In 1966, Applewhite was hired as a music teacher at the University of St. Thomas, a private Catholic college in Houston. He sang fifteen roles with the Houston Grand Opera before leaving in 1970, according to the *New York Times Magazine* profile.

But Balch said Applewhite was fired from St. Thomas following a scandalous relationship with a student.

The next year he was hired as director of music at St. Mark's Episcopal Church in Houston, where he stayed for a year before the disastrous and life-changing interview he and Nettles gave the *Houston Post.*

"I wouldn't have seen any preview of any of the cult business that finally happened," Tom Crow, an organist at the church told the *New York Times.* "He was a superb musician, a superb singer, and a super choir director."

He was, Crow insisted, "an extraordinarily gentle fellow."

Nettles' background is far less exotic—but her break from her past no less dramatic.

Born in 1928 and raised a Baptist, Louise Lu Trusdale Nettles was trained as a professional nurse, married, and raised four children in near obscurity in the Houston area. But her life slowly, inexorably began to change in the turbulent '60s.

Like many in those years of the so-called Age of Aquarius, Nettles cultivated an intense, almost religious interest in reincarnation, astrology, and mysticism. Unlike most others, she never abandoned it.

After she met the handsome, witty, and talented Applewhite, her destiny became even clearer, more urgent. With hardly a look back, or a tear shed, Nettles left her husband, and grown children to open the Christian Arts Center with Applewhite.

Nettles' astrological charts would presage some of the marvels Bo and Peep would preach to their followers. The cult's philosophical base was growing larger, and more alarming, with each day.

In 1974, shortly after they claimed to have "awakened" to the knowledge they had known each other in outer space and had been sent here to collect passengers for a flying saucer heading back, they reportedly made their first convert. It was a feat with both pathetic and hilarious, even disastrous consequences.

The first passenger booked on the flying saucer to peace and happiness was a housewife whose husband did not approve of his wife's leaving him—even for such a lofty reason as a ticket to heaven. According to Bo [Applewhite], in an attempt to retrieve his wife, the husband reported his car and the family credit card stolen.

There was a further mix-up involving a rental car that was kept overtime by Bo and Peep.

Bo and Peep—or "The Two," as they alternately dubbed themselves—were arrested in Harlingen, Texas, in August 1974; Bo on car theft charges and Peep on a credit card count, which was later dropped.

The case took six months to come to trial,
when a public defender convinced him to
plead guilty. The sentence was four months.

"I now have two months credit due me,"
he good-naturedly told the *New York Times
Magazine.*

Jail time, if nothing else, gave Bo a lot of
time to think. By the time he was freed,
most of the cult philosophy had gelled. It
was no longer a mix of science-fiction fantasy and heavenly predictions. Bo's religious background was working its way into
the astrological ramblings.

In a statement the cult would finally post
on the Internet some twenty-two years
later, Bo recorded the heart of his fool-
hardy philosophy.

"What religions have sought to understand since the beginning of their origin is
what is above the human level of existence," Bo wrote. "Most have taught that if
an individual lives a 'good life' adoring
some savior, that he will inherit some
'heaven' after his death. If only it were that
simple."

Instead, Bo proposed a far more complicated approach to the "higher level."

"A member of the next kingdom finds favor with one who is willing to endure all of the necessary growing pains of weaning himself totally from his human condition. Members of the next kingdom are no more confined to human limitations than butterflies to caterpillar limitations."

Translated: Somebody up there is watching you, from a hovering flying saucer no less, and he'll be your ticket to ride to the heavens. You may leave your body behind, but your spirit will soar.

Something else was happening with Bo and Peep's philosophy. Bo was beginning to draw a comparison between his "higher level" beings and Jesus Christ.

"He . . . came to know that he had incarnated for the express purpose of telling and showing, even to the point of proof, that the next kingdom can be entered by overcoming the human aspects and literally converting into a 'man' or creature of that next kingdom—the kingdom of his Father—one who is already a member of that kingdom."

The Christian references are all through his 1974 jailhouse "statement."

But the startlingly new aspect is no less than Bo's pronouncement that he, in fact, is the new Jesus sent here to Earth to lead his flock back to heaven. It was the logical, the only conclusion he could have drawn from those first seeds of power planted in his fertile mind by the nurse who cared for him.

"There are two individuals here now who have also come from the next kingdom, incarnate as humans, awakened, and will soon demonstrate the same proof of overcoming death," Bo wrote, referring to himself and Peep.

"They are 'sent' from that kingdom by the 'Father' to bear the same truth that was Jesus'. This is like a repeat performance, except this time, by two (a man and a woman) to restate the truth Jesus bore, restore its accurate meaning, and again show that any individual who seeks that kingdom will find it through the same process."

He promised the "re-statement" or "demonstration" will happen within months.

Translation—and this group needed nothing if not translation of their near impossible-to-understand jargon— The big flying saucer in the sky is coming soon, so have your bags packed and ready. Get rid of the old and prepare for the new. We're traveling light.

"The two who are the 'actors' in this 'theater' are in the meantime doing all they can to relate this truth as accurately as possible so that when their bodies recover from their 'dead' state (resurrection) and they leave (UFOs) those left behind will have clearly understood the formula."

Through all the mumbo jumbo, the central message became all too clear: a UFO is waiting to pick up earthling stragglers ready to ascend to the heavens.

The message, the urgency, was a culmination of four years of thought and talk and mutual cheerleading. Yet when the act was ready for the road, Bo and Peep were surprisingly, oddly, sheepish about their first foray into the public.

"There was a little Episcopal church in Spokane, Washinton," Bo told the *New York Times Magazine*.

"We wrote on the register at the church what our mission was and then ran. Next we told a Baptist preacher in Oklahoma City and he threw us out. He said he had

had Moses and Elijah there and didn't need anyone else. After that, we wrote little notes about our mission and dropped them in the strangest places all over the nation. I'm sure people have found them in the middle of their Bibles."

Eventually Bo and Peep hit Southern California where a psychic guru named Clarence King had heard about them. He arranged for his students and friends to attend a meeting with The Two at the house of Joan Culpepper in April 1975.

Eighty people crowded inside and when Bo and Peep had finished their evangelical-like tale, more than a third of their listeners were ready to go.

It was the cults first big success at recruitment, with many more to follow. At its height, the cult reportedly swelled to one hundred members.

Culpepper recalled the extraordinary meeting to the *New York Times Magazine* a year later:

"I really didn't like them and was very skeptical. I didn't buy a lot of the things they said. But an extraordinary thing happened when I was listening to Bo.

"It was as if a strong force came down over my mind and shut off my critical sense. I think The Two have strong psychic powers and the ability to brainwash people."

Bo boasted proudly after the meeting: "There are a lot of advanced souls in Southern California."

Another meeting attendant, Todd Berger, a film editor who joined, and then left, the cult, described the successful recruitment in far simpler terms.

"UFOs fascinate me and I just wanted to take a trip on a spacecraft," he told the *New York Times Magazine*.

The Two found dozens of others just like Todd Berger, fascinated by flying saucers, lost in their own hallow lives, eager for excitement and purpose.

Bo and Peep were the perfect shepherds for these lost souls, and they led their sheep up and down the West Coast and through the Southwest during 1974 and 1975.

The handsome charismatic leader knew full well his power by this time.

"There's a lesson to be learned by watching sheep," Bo reportedly said in one

sermon to followers he'd led to an idyllic
mountain field in southern Colorado during
the summer of 1975. "One will jump over
an imaginary fence and pretty soon they'll
all be jumping over the fence—all equally
convinced the fence is really there."

It was in a small seacoast town in Oregon
where the cult burst into the national con-
sciousness with a frightening pounce.

"A score of persons from a small Oregon
town have disappeared," Walter Cronkite
calmly informed the nation on October 8,
1975. "It's a mystery whether they've been
taken on a so-called trip to eternity . . . or
simply been taken."

What followed not only stunned the
nation, it fanned a UFO fever that had raged
since the '50s.

"Rocket ships from outer space. Buck
Rogers fantasy, or is it?" the CBS correspondent intoned in front of the motel where
the meeting had taken place.

"Today, there is a group of earthlings who
believe they're on their way to a rendezvous with such a ship for a trip to the
unknown. Here along the cloud-covered
coast near Newport, Oregon, a mysterious

couple appeared three weeks ago, circulating a flier proclaiming a UFO. would soon be ready to take whoever would follow them to another life, another world. They held meetings, one at this motel, to recruit voyagers."

The correspondent reported the recruits, the "vanished people," had given away everything—including kids—and all of their material belongs, including property, cars, boats, and money, "and just left."

"Twenty or more faithful are now apparently headed for the lonely prairie of eastern Colorado."

But Bo and Peep remained mysterious to the nation at large. They were rarely identified in the mainstream press, including in Associated Press and the *Newsweek* articles that followed the infamous recruitment meeting on September 14, in Waldport, Oregon.

Though the meeting could have been considered Bo and Peep's second successful recruitment, the leaders seemed to remain even mysterious to followers willing to give up their lives to hitchhike on a spaceship.

"It may seem hokey or sacrilegious to you,"

one newcomer wrote to her mother after that meeting. "But believe me it was neither. The stress of their whole talk was a message given to us almost 2,000 years ago by Jesus, and this is victory over death—ascension."

Bo and Peep's ragtag band popped up in a smattering of news accounts thereafter, breathlessly reporting the odd strangers' whereabouts and doings.

By this time, Bo and Peep's crusade had been given a name: The Human Individual Metamorphosis—HIM.

"The Northern California recruits are thought to have journeyed to Mount Madonna Park in Santa Clara County after a meeting in Sunnyvale, south of San Francisco, about a month ago, San Mateo County Assistant DA Margaret Kemp said yesterday," the Associated Press reported on October 6, 1975.

"It is not known where they went from there, she said. They reportedly were equipped only with camping gear.

"A park ranger said he had seen three or four middle-aged persons wandering around looking for UFOs, but that he had seen no large gathering."

The news service reported two HIM meetings had been held in Oregon; three in Northern California.

An advertisement that ran in the *San Jose Mercury-News* in advance for one meeting read:

"The opportunity is here, when we as humans can fully evolve into a higher being. There is now on this planet two people from the higher level [UFO beings] here to help us and many others with this transition."

Advertisements for the Waldport meeting were similarly enticing—and maddenly vague:

"If you have ever entertained the idea that there may be a real, physical level beyond the Earth's confines, you will want to attend this meeting," the poster for that infamous meeting urged.

Some two hundred people turned up at the Bayshore Inn that September 14 to hear what the couple calling themselves The Two had to say. The message was simple, and startling:

A spaceship would transport them to the "next evolutionary level" within months.

When The Two left town shortly after, twenty-three recruits vanished with them, abandoning families, friends and worldly possessions to head to Colorado, where they believed the UFO would land.

Waldport never forgot the visitors who came alone, and left with so many. They wondered even then what kind of weird spaced-out cult had blown into town on the winds of hope and fear, mixed up together.

• "People just disappeared," remembers Carol van Strum, who works at a bookstore and restaurant called Canyon Way in neighboring Newport. "Mostly the attitude back then was like, wow, you know, that's weird."

John Anderson, who worked at a local radio station and recalled The Two walking in one day to promote their upcoming meeting at the Bayshore Inn. The station's popular talk-show host, now dead, put them on the air, Anderson said, and soon people were calling with questions—first from Portland and Salem, then from around the country.

The response surprised everybody, and troubled a few.

Like others who encountered The Two, Anderson remembers the couple as "very unassuming." With their short hair and neat appearances they stood out in those mellow times. They looked straight when everyone else did not.

It wasn't that Waldport had never attracted anyone rootless or lost. Its woodsy environs attracted its fair share of people seeking alternate lifestyles, and many of those who left with The Two were believed to be newcomers or people just passing through.

Robert Rubin abandoned his house to join the group but returned about a year later and now runs a health food store.

Rubin was twenty-six when he heard the message of The Two at the Bayshore Inn. He gave away ten acres of land to join Applewhite and Nettles, and followed them for about six months on a penniless tour of the country.

"We went all around the United States," he told the *Oregonian* newspaper. "We tested the (charitability of the local) churches. We had nothing. We left everything behind, no money, no anything."

Annie Miller, then twenty-three, ran away with The Two, but later left the group to become a jewelry-maker in Santa Fe. Another local man chased after the group to reclaim his wife.

But no one filed any missing person reports at the time, according to the local authorities and media and two police investigators sent to check out the Bayshore Inn meeting concluded that no laws were broken.

The disappearance was strange, mysterious even. But eventually, not very bothersome. The time, 1975, was an era when hippies and lumberjacks peaceably comingled and one local grocer handed out free bones to dogs who followed their owners inside.

When another follower of The Two hitchhiked into town from California two months later to hold another meeting, this time at the Newport City Hall, newspaper accounts show that the new audience was filled with concerned relatives whose questions were dismissed as "unimportant" by the twenty-year-old speaker, identified at the time as Brian Wallenstein.

The young man said he was supplied with food and other earthly needs by a spaceship; nevertheless, he left a coffee can in the back of the room for donations.

The group swelled from the original Waldport adherents to several hundred by the time they reached Chicago late in 1975 or early in 1976. The Two preached a lot of spaced-out, trippy philosophy—and demanded a renouncement of a former life, but little else.

Certainly not suicide.

"No one would have gone along if they had mentioned suicide," Robert Rubin said. "What they did say is they predicted they would be killed within months and resurrected in three days and then would come back for the rest of us. We were supposed to go through a change to join them—but not suicide.

"I believed it for a while," he said. "But the timetable kept slipping. What they said would happen in months didn't happen."

Rubin and most of the followers dropped away; Rubin eventually returned to Waldport. He said he doesn't regret the experience. It had been "a real valuable experience in terms of developing attitudes and not being uptight," he said.

Other new recruits—those who stayed—also were impressed by the message preached by Bo and Peep, and the personal freedom the pair gave them. The recruits believed the weird message from Bo and Peep, or Him and Her, or The Two—one that mixed religion and astrology and an obsession with UFOs—was part of a greater plan they might not understand. But they weren't the ones who had to know the details.

That was what Bo and Peep did; they kept the fire alive. They knew the time and place and method to reach the "higher level."

Part of their method of keeping recruits close was the constant tantalization of the imminent arrival of the beloved spaceship that would save them from the world.

The date of arrival was never quite clear—and was the reason why so many finally defected from those early wanderings.

"We have never stated the time," Bo argued. "It is not that we are hiding any-thing. Heavens, if we knew the exact month we would leave, we would say it."

Through all the flim-flam about when the flying saucer would arrive to bail out true believers, Bo and Peep kept a high level of spiritual cheerleading, emphasizing over and over that the only way to make the outer space trip to a "higher level" was to shed all the old pretensions and possessions.

The early enthusiasm of recruits soon faded for some. It seemed inevitable.

Through the early days of recruitment from Oregon, California, Colorado, Arizona, and New Mexico, Bo and Peep didn't bother keeping very close touch with the flock—a sure-fire way to lose foundering souls ready to fly away in search of another promise of happiness and peace.

Worse, some of the original recruits became downright hostile. Like Joan Culpepper—whose home hosted the seminal meeting held by The Two. By 1976, Culpepper had become one of Bo and Peep's biggest critics. She accused her former shepherds of fleecing her for $433 for the price of a spaceship ride she never got to take. A complaint was filed, but no charges ever resulted.

Through it all, Bo and Peep persevered,

unfazed by either the attention, adoration, suspicion, or scorn.

"Some people are like lemmings, who rush in a pack into the sea and drown themselves," Bo said about his dropouts.

"Many migrate to the West Coast. They join any movement—self-discipline, this kind of meditation, that kind of mediation, this kind of strict diet, that kind of diet. Then they go half way around the world to try another movement and it is just look, look, look, look."

For the followers who stuck out the endless meanderings and watchful waitings for a spaceship that never landed, it was just blind faith that kept them tagging along after their middle-aged shepherds.

"There were a lot of Biblical references to what they did," Rubin said. "Something out of Revelations. . . . They said when they did certian things, a few days later they'd be taken off in spaceships."

In all the seemingly aimless wanderings of Bo and Peep's flock, there was, in fact, method in the madness.

For the most part, the comings and goings of the cult were revealed by a pair of young, energetic scholars from the University of Montana who infiltrated the group in 1975.

Their names were Robert Balch and David Taylor.

It is primarily from their firsthand account that people learned the structure, habits, philosophy—and disappointments— of that first-formed band of believers.

Balch also came to know enough about Bo to learn of his earlier days, when he suffered a mental breakdown that landed him in a hospital where Peep worked, and of his bisexuality that continued even after Bo moved back in disgrace to Texas.

"Six weeks after the Waldport disappearance, we joined the UFO group after attending a meeting held by about twenty followers in Arizona," the pair wrote in a *Psychology Today* report in October 1976.

"We both had special interest in the group. One of us [Balch] had been studying the sociological aspects of metaphysics and the occult, while the other [Taylor] had done his master's thesis on recruitment and conversion in Sun Moon's Unification Church."

The pair recounted that at the point they joined the cult, Bo and Peep had just two weeks before left their flock in Oklahoma, supposedly to "get in tune with the Father."

Bo and Peep were not ones to keep very close contact with their flock.

"When we met [the cult], the UFO people were heading for Oakland, where they expected to rejoin The Two for something they called 'the Demonstration,' " the pair wrote.

The followers briefed the new recruits on just who Bo and Peep were: "like Jesus, they would be martyred, and three and a half days later, would demonstrate death over come by rising from the dead and leaving the earth in a cloud of light, which Bo and Peep called the Biblical term for a UFO."

The followers hoped this flight to heaven would take off from Oakland. When the band from Oklahoma arrived, they were joined by seventy-five other members from St. Louis. But the elusive Bo and Peep were a no-show for their own "demonstration."

The flock, never numbering more than one hundred, Batch and Taylor contended, despite Bo's boast of having two hundred followers, was left to "wander aimlessly along the California coast" for about a week, the infiltrators said.

There was always some dispute about the money-making possibilities for Bo and Peep as cult leaders.

But Bo and Peep maintained in interviews that any money matters were settled among the followers, often pooled in common funds for use by everyone.

"We don't have any bills," Bo told the *New York Times Magazine.* "We live in tents, or in motels when the rooms have been given to us."

Peep added: "We receive donations."

Bo told the interviewer their pennies came from heaven.

"We've done whatever is required to sustain our needs," Bo added. "Whenever we are in communication with the next level, our needs are supplied."

The infiltrators found out much about what it took to be a follower of such delusional leaders.

"Many of the UFO group were attracted by the short-term nature of their commitment,"

they noted, ". . . The Two's followers expected
to enter the Kingdom of Heaven within
months. Many of them set personal deadlines
for the pickup.

"The 'process' required a complete break
with the past," the scholars wrote.

"Each true seeker must at one time walk
out of the door of his life, leaving behind
career, security, every loved one, and every
single attachment in order to go through
the remaining needed experiences necessary to totally wean him from his needs at
the human level.

"A few followers did give up prestigious
jobs and expensive home, but most had few
material or emotional ties to conventional
life."

There was a short but stifling list of No's—
no sex, no drugs, no liquor, no tobacco, no
kids.

Children are "not eligible for the space
flight because the decision to go must be
made by each individual," Bo told his *New
York Times Magazine* interviewer.

They claimed to have known nothing
about members who gave up their kids to
join.

One man sold his home in Oregon for five dollars, they recounted. It had been unbelievably simple.

"For me it was easy," he told the new recruits. "I'm single. I just had some property to which I never felt any attachment anyway."

Another recruit, a Southwest artist and former encounter group leader, admitted:

"I gave up a lot to come on this trip, man. I gave up my record collection, a set of tools, my old lady. But it's not the first record collection I've given up. It's not the first set of tools. And I've had eight old ladies."

Beyond the requirement to shed their past life and all its material accoutrements, the recruits had very little else the cult demanded of them. Socializing within the group was discouraged and there were no games, songs, public confessions, or rituals of any kind.

There were a few stable features: Everyone was assigned a partner shortly after joining up. Usually, the partner was someone from the opposite sex.

Partners would help each other by acting

as mirrors, recruits were told. They were to simply help each other reach that "higher level."

But there was also strict, almost prudish rules of behavior.

"Sexual relationships and even close friendships between partners were discouraged not only because they were too human, but because they held back the friction necessary to make one aware of his humanness," Balch and Taylor wrote.

"As one member told us: 'It's not a comfortable relationship by Earth standards, but it's good growth.'"

Yet the frugality was too much for others.

"After three months without an orgasm, I decided that this trip was not for me," one woman told the *New York Times Magazine*.

Perhaps in emulation of their leaders, many of the "seekers" changed their names.

"In two months, one girl changed her name from Starry to Sun to Asa, and finally to Christian," Balch and Taylor found.

There was little resemblance to other stricter, more regimented religious cults. Members admitted they were told to try not to stand out in a crowd, to get too much attention. They wanted to appear bland, and just blend in, or at worst, "just look like another bunch of kooks," one said.

Few worried about whether their cherished leaders, or their lofty mission, was a hoax.

"If nothing else," one recruit said, "The process has helped me be a better human."

"New members experienced nothing remotely resembling the indoctrination provided in other religious cults like the Unification Church," Balch and Taylor wrote.

"The UFO people spent most of their time trying to establish contact with the Father in Heaven. . . . In a refreshing contrast to other religious cults, the UFO group was almost totally noncoercive. Free choice was the cornerstone of Human Individual Metamorphosis."

But all this freewheeling was frustrating for some of the followers.

During one public meeting, a follower compared the group's aimless wandering to pinballs bouncing from stop to stop, Balch and Taylor reported.

"Their spokesman agreed," they said. "But

at each point we have the choice to bounce or not."

To the outside world, the wandering band of "UFO people" was bizarre, scary even.

When the HIM followers set up a post-office box in Wauconda, Illinois, about fifty miles northwest of Chicago in October 1975, the locals described them as "suspicious-acting" people arriving in cars with California and Oregon license plates.

It was the furthest east the group wandered. They spent about a week camped at the Chain O'Lakes State Park near Fox Lake in suburban Lake County.

"Mrs. Charlene Petrovic of Waukegan said she watched the group for several days while she and her husband camped at the state park," one Associated Press account related.

Bo and Peep, these New Age pied pipers, didn't care about the rubes, or their reactions. They cared about getting recruits, and keeping their traveling show on the road.

Their bizarre metaphors and veiled threats of doom were either passed off as ridiculous or described as prophetic.

"Light is coming into this planet," the

group told a 1976 New Mexico gathering, according to the *Santa Fe Reporter.*

"An opportunity is offered to humans. Those ready can graduate from the garden. You must leave behind loved ones, security, possessions. This time is known as the harvest."

One couple even gave their baby up for adoption and signed on, according to a 1975 *Los Angeles Times* article.

"What it really is is the story of a traveling asylum," former member Todd Berger told the *Times.*

In the late 1970s, Applewhite and Nettles came into an inheritance totaling at least $300,000, ending their camping phase.

Newly rich, the group rented houses in Denver and Texas and became extremely secretive.

But when they were New Age nomads, Bo and Peep once let a recruit leave the encampment in 1975 to tell his story to the world. Paul Groll, then thirty-two, was the one selected to share his experiences.

His account showed that followers were just as fascinated by Bo and Peep as astounded strangers.

"I just felt drawn to them," Groll told *Time* magazine in 1975. "You could feel the goodness."

Groll gave another fascinating picture of life inside the camping cult.

He said about four dozen people moved between a site in the Wyoming rockies to a ranch in northern Texas. Unarmed guards were sentries at the perimeter of the compound, he said.

Unlike the two sociologists, Groll described a rigid life inside the cult.

Bo and Peep have "thousands of rules," he said. "But they never force anyone to do anything." During one three-month phase, members constantly wore hoods over their heads and peered out through mirrored eye slits for no apparent reason.

The usual uniform, as described by Groll, was a brightly colored windbreaker over a jumpsuit. Gloves were worn at all times. There was minimal communication: yes, no, or I don't know, were the usual verbal exchanges. Everything else that needed to be said was written.

They studied the Bible, but could watch TV newscasts and read newspapers—if only to compare and contrast the values of the camp with those of the outside world. The newspapers' obituaries, stock market reports, and sports pages were cut out, a censorship needed to keep the followers in focus, Groll contended.

At the two daily meals, which Bo and Peep called "lab experiments," a blackboard would list "formulas" specifying the menu: PA for potatoes, CA for cake. The food would have to be eaten with care to reduce noise.

Bo and Peep shopped for food and supplies personally, paying in cash.

They once told recruits they "didn't have any need to wonder" about money, Groll said.

Groll never once believed he or any of the other recruits were comparable to the tragic followers of Jim Jones.

"Anyone can walk away. We just have to turn from a caterpillar into a butterfly and then we'll be ready to leave," he said enigmatically.

There were scattered recruitment meetings as far away as Vermont in 1975.

That spring, three members of the cult—

without Bo and Peep—visited Goddard
College in Plainfield, Vermont, former student Dania Kara recalled. Kara describes
herself now as a "professional psychic."

"They had fliers out, announcing their
arrival," she recalled. "There was only about
three of them and only about four students
showed up. They didn't have any logic to
what they were talking about. And this one
girl said, 'Well, that's the beauty of it. I'm
losing logic. I can't add anymore.' That blew
me away. She was losing the ability to add.
It was sort of spooky. They were just drifting."

All of the media attention finally drove
the group underground.

Oddly, the astute Balch and his fellow
researcher never found much to worry
about in either Bo or Peep when they wrote
about the group in *Psychology Today.*

"Bo, who did most of the talking during
their public meetings, was articulate, witty,
and charismatic. He had a remarkable
knack for creating with words what Walt
Disney called the 'plausible impossible.'
Peep was equally well respected by those
who knew her.

" 'I've only met a few really powerful people in my life,' said one of their followers. 'It was obvious that they were locked into some energy source that gave them extraordinary powers.'

"In spite of their charisma, we saw few signs of the personality cult that usually springs up around such spiritual leaders. During most of the public meetings we observed, The Two were mentioned only in passing and occasionally not at all. To their followers, Bo and Peep were more like wise parents than Messiahs from the next world."

The pair even seemed to have a sense of humor, the scholars noted.

"The Two told their followers that one of the few things they would take with them to the next level was their sense of humor. They once joked about wearing bull's eyes to the Demonstration to make things easier for any would-be assassins. Even their names, Bo and Peep, were a satirical comment on our society names, and on their own roles as space-age shepherds."

There were rare moments when Bo and Peep seemed surprisingly human, Balch and Taylor said.

"Once while they were staying in Las Vegas, one of their followers happened across Peep standing in front of a row of slot machines just as she hit the jackpot.

"'Look,' she said sheepishly. 'See how the Father is letting us win.'"

By 1980, another dramatic change was about to take place for Bo and Peep. These inveterate teachers of metamorphosis were about to do just that, again. But it would be in secret.

With their new inheritance, and plenty of unwanted media and law enforcement attention, it seemed safer to simply drop out of sight.

For the next decade, there would be little heard from The Two. Soon, there would just one.

Chapter

5

CULTS, CRAZIES, and CALIFORNIA

California has the reputation of being the nation's flakiest state, having nurtured a mindboggling variety of kooks and killers over the years.

The Golden State's bad reputation went into full blossom in the 1960s—those turbulent years of the Vietnam War, political and social upheaval sparked by disenchanted youth, and the free-love Age of Aquarius.

Almost overnight, it seemed like California was being blamed for everything that was wrong with America, every problem perceived to be tearing down the great moral fabric of the nation.

The wacky religious cults, the wide-eyed serial killers, the earthy-crunchy New Age gurus, the stalkers and the nutjobs—were all happily living on the Left Coast.

And who could argue? Timothy Leary was up in San Francisco urging American youth to "Tune In, Turn On, and Drop Out." Hollywood was seen as a cesspool of corruption fueled by a booze-fueled, sex-mad entertainment industry which supplied America with its movies and TV.

Who could forget Woody Allen's shock at the hedonistic, self-absorbed coke-sniffing party guests at an appalling Hollywood shindig in *Annie Hall*?

But while California's reputation really didn't start suffering until four decades ago, its magnet-like pull to thousands of colorful, questionable characters began two centuries back.

Noted *Los Angeles Times* columnist Peter King wrote that most of California's most famous weirdos migrated from other states, only to bloom into notoriety after they arrived.

William Money made his mark as the first of California's legendary cult czars.

Money was a robust Scotsman who came to Los Angeles in 1840 only after—according to his own oft-told story—he received marching orders from Jesus while standing on a New York City street corner.

Eight years later, more than 80,000 opportunists from all over the world flooded California with picks, axes, explosives, and dreams of endless riches when gold was discovered. Following them like scavenger fish were prostitutes, bootleggers, fundamentalists, golddiggers, thieves, killers, and other flotsam and jetsam all seeking their own piece of the action,

In 1935, journalist Bruce Bliven wrote about California: "Here is the world's prize collection of cranks, semi-cranks, placid creatures whose bovine expressions show that each of them is studying, without much hope of success, to be a high-grade moron, angry or ecstatic exponent of food fads, sunbathing, ancient Greek costumes, diaphragm-breathing. And the imminent second coming of Christ."

A few years later, historian John Steven McGroarty would note in a more conservative tone:

"Los Angeles is the most celebrated of all incubators of new creeds, codes of ethics, philosophies—no day passes without the birth of something this nature never heard of before.

"It is a breeding place and a rendezvous of freak religions. But this is because its winters are mild, thus luring the pale people of thought to its sunny gates."

One of these so-called "freak religions" was the WKFL Foundation of the World, established in 1948 by Krishna Venta, a former boilermaker from Berkeley who had changed his name from Francis Pencovic.

WKFL stood for wisdom, knowledge, faith, and love—the backbone of Venta's teachings.

Claiming he was created by God in a Himalayan valley without human parents—Venta began a colony of fifty-three adults and kids in the stunning Chatsworth Valley in Ventura County.

He preached that smoking was good for one's health and that man had been brought to Earth thousands of years earlier on twelve large spaceships powered by high-energy "cosmic" fuel.

Marshall Applewhite, the leader of the Heaven's Gate cult, is shown in an undated image made available March 28, 1997. Thirty-nine members of Heaven's Gate committed mass suicide in their home near San Diego on March 26, 1997. (AP PHOTO/APTV)

This photo of Marshall Applewhite and Bonnie Lu Trusdale Nettles was taken in October 1975, in Harlingen, Texas. (UPI/CORBIS BETTMAN)

Drawings that were on display at a 1994 Heaven's Gate enrollment meeting included "Globe with Ring," which depicts the cult's view of the other dimension. (SEVANS PHOTOGRAPHY/SPECIAL TO THE STAR TRIB)

A drawing of the spaceship that the cult believed was coming to pick them up. (SEVANS PHOTOGRAPHY/SPECIAL TO THE STAR TRIB)

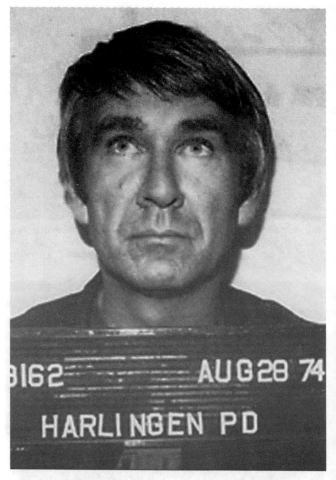

162   AUG 28 74

HARLINGEN PD

Marshall Applewhite is shown in this 1974 police mug shot taken after he
was arrested for auto theft in Harlingen, Texas.
(AP PHOTO/HARLINGEN POLICE)

Only On
ACTION NEWS

Frame grab from a videotape showing cult leader Marshall Applewhite beckoning followers to leave Earth. The tape and a suicide note came from a minister in Michigan who received it by Federal Express, KCBS-TV said. (AP PHOTO/WTOL-TV and KCBS-TV)

Moving trucks wait to be loaded with furniture and other belongings, March 28, 1997, from the mansion in Rancho Santa Fe rented by the Heaven's Gate cult. (AP PHOTO/MARK J. TERRILL)

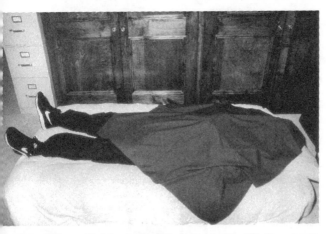

A photograph provided by the San Diego County Sheriff's Department shows the position of one of the 39 bodies discovered at the Heaven's Gate compound in Rancho Santa Fe, California. (AP PHOTO/HO)

San Diego and Los Angeles County Medical Examiner personnel place some of the 39 victims of the mass suicide onto a truck for transport to the morgue. (AP PHOTO/MARK J. TERRILL)

Looking for:

The next world

The pleasant, middle-aged Texans who, on page four of consent prepare for a one-way trip "OUT" to the "next level above human"

Frame grab from Channel 7 Eyewitness News (WABC-TV) of the headline of a *New York Times Magazine* profile of Marshall Applewhite and Bonnie Nettles from the mid '70s. (WABC-TV)

"I may as well say it! I am Christ!" announced Venta, who began referring to himself as "The Voice."

He instructed his followers not to wear shoes, cut their hair, or wear anything except long robes until world peace had been achieved.

Attempting to perform their civic duty, many of the cultists joined the local volunteer fire department. That had its problems when there were large, out-of-control fires to be fought because the cultists refused to put on shoes or change from their robes.

The cult came to an explosive end ten years later on December 10, 1958, when two followers, convinced Venta was having regular sex trysts with their wives, set off a bomb made with twenty sticks of dynamite.

Venta, his killers, and six others perished in the explosion which could be heard more than twenty miles away.

As one cult died, another was about to be born. In 1960, a young Philadelphia car salesman named Jack Rosenberg quit his job, left his wife and four young kids and headed west with a second, secret wife.

Changing his name to Werner Hans

Erhard, he moved to San Francisco where he began a successful foray into what he labeled the "mind business"—selling motivational and self-awareness books. Soon he created his own self-awareness course—EST, short for Erhard Seminars Training—and began leading two-week "training seminars" in Big Sur.

EST spread like wildfire with celebrities including Diana Ross, Valerie Harper, and John Denver taking the pricy lessons. Hundreds of volunteers and young people moved to Erhard's sprawling estate to serve their master.

His controversial training sessions consisted of boot-camp–like tactics including group leaders screaming obscenities at students, bathroom breaks being banned and emotional breakdowns being encouraged. All in the name of "getting in touch with one's self."

EST was even parodied in the Hollywood comedy "Bob and Carol and Ted and Alice" in which two middle-aged couples try to relive their youth by going into therapy, doing drugs, and wife-swapping.

Erhard's EST program was a rousing

success through the early '80s, but then hit a curve when the touchy-feely guru began being dogged by the Internal Revenue Service over several tax issues. In the early '90s, Erhard was hit by allegations that he had physically abused his second wife, Ellen, and sexually abused two of his daughters. CBS's *60 Minutes* did a scathing report on him. Apparently, unable to apply his own meditative principals to himself and chill out, Erhard left his followers high and dry by fleeing the United States. No criminal charges were ever filed against him.

In the early '60s, the same canyon that served the weird Krishna Venta's home became the temporary residence of Charles Manson.

Manson was a pale, stringy-haired ex-con from Ohio who had headed west in quest to conquer the music business with his compositions.

But with insipid, tuneless songs like "Garbage Pail" nobody was biting. So Manson headed in another direction. With his deep-set hypnotic eyes, a charismatic rap, and the promise of great drugs and groovy vibes, he lured impressionable crops of young hippies to follow him to the sprawling and scenic Spahn Movie Ranch outside Los Angeles. Spahn was where hundreds of action movies and TV shows were routinely cranked out and the Manson "kids" were constantly running into famous actors and actresses.

Among those the clan bumped into was Lon Chaney Jr., by then a tragically hopeless alcoholic grinding out his final picture, "The Female Bunch"—a sex-filled, low-budget flick about a cult of buxom B-girls who hate men.

At Spahn, Manson led his eager brood in week-long LSD sessions and sex orgies in which he ordered his young women *and* men to submit to every carnal activity imaginable.

It was the time of Free Love and Flower Power, with places like Haight-Ashbury and Los Angeles becoming meccas for the young who yearned to explore their freedom, through sex, drugs, and rock 'n' roll.

With a virtually bottomless supply of marijuana, acid, cocaine, and heroin, Manson transformed his doe-eyed innocents into drug-fueled zombies.

Under this haze they would do anything for him—and did. The women sold their bodies as prostitutes to supply Manson with pocket cash, while the men burglarized houses, shoplifted, and robbed.

Manson became obsessed with the Beatles song "Helter Skelter," which he said predicted an inevitable black-white racial war that would tear apart America.

"Now is the time for Helter Skelter!" Manson proclaimed as he sent out a small army of followers to break into famed movie director Roman Polanski's L.A. home on August 9, 1969, and help launch the war.

Using carving knives and blades, the gang butchered five people including Polanski's pregnant wife, blonde actress Sharon Tate. In a gory afterthought, the young killers dipped their fingers into the victims' bloody wounds and smeared the word "Pig" and other declarations on the walls.

Two nights later, the youthful butchers struck again, this time hacking up wealthy grocery store owners Leno and Rosemary LaBianca near Los Feliz. Manson and four others were sentenced to life behind bars.

As Manson's cult disbanded, a young group of urban terrorists called the Symbionese Liberation Army grabbed headlines by kidnapping and brainwashing newspaper heiress Patty Hearst, who would go on to help them rob banks.

Hearst was later freed and the SLA's principal leaders blown away in a fierce gun battle. But the SLA didn't die—and in fact, came back with a vengeance five years later in a bizarre plot to spring Charles Manson from jail.

The plan by the SLA and a few diehard members of the fragmented Manson gang was ultimately foiled. Cops discovered the groups had spent two years raising two million dollars for the operation through a series of credit card scams and bank robberies.

The proposed bust-out was to have involved a daring helicopter attack on the prison where Manson was housed.

The '70s were also witness to the horrifying Jonestown mass suicide in the jungles of Guyana in which 913 people committed suicide—or were forced to commit suicide—at the orders of cult leader Jim Jones.

And while the November 18, 1978, horror occurred light years away in terms of location, California got much of the blame because Jones and his Peoples Temple Church had gained prominence in the San Francisco area a few years earlier.

Jones grew up in Lynn, Indiana, the son of a Ku Klux Klansman, eventually breaking away to preach in Indianapolis. In 1955, he opened a church called the Peoples Temple, a combination soup kitchen and second-hand clothing store.

His firebrand preaching style made him an excellent fundraiser and soon he opened two nursing homes and began buying up real estate. But some creative accounting got him into trouble with the IRS. As he battled with the taxmen, Jones became convinced that he—and the larger world—faced disaster. Or as Jones described it, an "atomic holocaust."

Reading a magazine article which listed the world's nine safest places to hide from nuclear fallout, Jones noticed Ukriah, California, 150 miles north of San Francisco. Fearing the world would end on July 15, 1967, Jones moved with 150 of his disciples to Ukriah. Even though the date passed without incident, Jones and his Peoples Temple decided to stay put—settling in the nearby picturesque hamlet of Redwood Valley.

With his charismatic preaching and show-biz style, Jones flourished in California, soon finding himself commanding as many as five thousand disciples. He began telling people he was God and disciplining those who disobeyed him with a large whip.

He cruelly flayed a four-year-old boy who refused to eat his food until the youngster threw up. Then, according to the recollections of ex-members, the boy was forced to eat his own vomit. Jones also began assigning sex partners to his members and often had disciples he desired—men and women— come to his room for sweaty sex sessions.

One newly pubescent young girl Jones feared was on her way to becoming a lesbian felt his wrath—getting the wack of his large oak paddle seventy-five times on her bare buttocks until they "looked like hamburger meat," the girl's father testified later.

As Jones' questionable morals and

financial standings slipped, government officials, acting on tips, began an investigation of the Peoples Temple. Jones fled with his flock to the South American country of Guyana, where he had leased 824 acres for his followers to farm and grow fruits and vegetables.

But the change in climate didn't signal a change in Jones, who still ruled through intimidation, keeping the beatings and sex abuse going.

It became so apparent something was wrong that U.S. Congressman Leo Ryan went down to investigate.

Jones, knowing the jig was about up, had Ryan and other factfinders shot dead and then ordered his masses to swallow cyanide-laced Kool-Aid. According to government testimony, some of the disciples who decided they didn't want to end their lives were given no choice. They were either force fed or beaten to death.

The Jonestown massacre stunned the northern California region because most of the disciples had relatives they had left behind to make their last journey. To this day, the Jonestown horror remains one of

the darkest moments in world history and it
is irreversibly linked to California.

If religious zealots and faddish cultists
weren't enough, California was also
plagued by some of the most bizarre serial
killers anywhere in the world.

The Zodiac Killer wiped out as many as
forty people in the Bay Area of San
Francisco over an eight-year period beginning in 1966. The maniac—whose twisted
trademark was striking by the light of the
full moon—has never been apprehended.

And there are others: the Night Stalker,
who police said murdered fourteen people
over thirteen months in the mid 1980s; and
the Hillside Strangler, accused of ten killings
in the Los Angeles area and Washington
State in the late 1970s.

The list of names went on: the Trailside
Slayer, the Skid Row Stabber, the Sunset
Slayer.

Psychiatrists have pointed out that
Californians should not feel that they are
thought of as a bunch of lunatics. Rather, it
is the social freedom California has always

been famous for that promotes the hundreds of different lifetsyles and movements in which disturbed people can flourish.

But the notion that California residents are flakes is still hard to shake off to this day. After O.J. Simpson's double murder trial ended in an acquittal, stunning most of the nation, numerous New York City lawyers came forward to say, "That couldn't have happened here."

In his recent book, *The Last Days of the Late, Great State of California*, veteran writer Curt Gentry raised several theories as to why the Left Coast became the place where cults and kooks have surfaced so prominently.

"In moving to California people wanted a new start; they shopped not only for a new job, new house, new furniture, new auto, new friends, but also for a new religion," Gentry said.

"Another explanation had it that California was so democratized, so lacking in a clearly defined society, that people craved something extra-exclusive.

"Still another thesis claimed there were so many other distractions in California life

that religion, to compete, had to be startling, sensational, different."

Religion is certainly a big entity in
California, with more than three hundred
different faiths throughout the state. Many
of them—those that might be considered
"fringe religions"—have thrived on keeping
low profiles, conducting their meetings in
private, and being very secretive about their
comings and goings.

And, as history has shown, those secrets
have led to misunderstandings, violence,
and mass death—by murder or suicide.

Chapter

6

BO AND PEEP MEET CYBERSPACE

Bo and Peep, the androgynous New Age Shepherds of the '70s, suddenly became fat cat gurus of the '80s, flush with unexpected, and considerable, wealth.

It couldn't have come at a better time.

The UFO nomads—alternately known as the UFO Cult, or the Human Individual Metamorphosis (HIM) or Heaven's Gate— were not the most welcome site to the small communities they visited in the late 1970s. They seemed to be hounded by unwanted media and police attention.

Besides running out of places to hide, they were down to the hardest core of recruits, far from the one hundred or so who joined up in 1975. Now, the outsiders they drew to their meetings never numbered more than a handful.

The cult groupies left first, disappointed there would be no quick arrival of the flying saucer destined to carry them away, disgusted with a life on the road.

Then, a financial windfall opened new doors.

With the infusion of $300,000—an inheritance reportedly belonging to one of the members but shared with the group—Bo and Peep gave up the campsites, the moldy tents, the battle with bugs, bears, and bad weather that had marked their vagabond wanderings in 1975 and 1976.

Gone also was the sheepish hustling and begging for free motel rooms, and handouts from storeowners sympathetic—or at least not completely turned off—by the strange-looking, weird-sounding crew.

Bo and Peep—Marshall Applewhite and Bonnie Lu Nettles—were finished with the desolate meandering about the American west in search of a place to rest, to look skyward without unfriendly, unwelcome stares from overweight campers in crumpled fishing hats and tin trailers.

With cash, the group rented houses in Denver and Texas. The flying saucer freaks found shelter at last—not in the spaceship that they still watched for, dreamed of and talked about incessantly. But in brick and mortar, behind doors and windows.

Grounded, an apocalyptic change also took place, a change that came about in secret over the 1980s and early 1990s.

Bo and Peep's newly rich crew went underground by 1980. It was as simple as that. They simply disappeared from view. Not so with their legacy, which was already part of the popular culture.

Bo even encouraged it.

Applewhite had a hand in the making of a fairly successful 1982 TV science-fiction thriller, called "Mysterious Two," that been pitched for an NBC series pilot.

"Evangelists John Forsythe and Priscilla Pointer are really aliens, brainwashing earthlings so that they can take over!" a description reads in the *The Psychotronic Video Guide* by Michael Weldon. "Only James Stephens knows what's going on."

Also starring in the boob-tube flick was Robert Englund, who two years later scared the pants off America playing the deformed, razor-clawed madman Freddy Kruger.

Just three years after the showing of the TV movie, Peep died of liver cancer.

The passing of Bo's muse, the co-founder of his deluded dream world, slipped away with nary a word at the time. Eleven years after her death, it was almost casually noted by Bo, who began calling himself Do and who memorialized Peep as Ti.

In the transcript of a videotape made by Bo on September 29, 1996—and soon after released on the Internet—the aging leader paid credit to the former nurse and astrologer whose deluded visions and astral obsession helped launch and define the cult's hopeless mission.

Nothing is said of how she died, or where, or with whom.

It is an awkward good-bye. And a cold one. As always, the reference began with him.

"And here I am, I'm Do, Do of Ti and Do, of the little religious 'UFO Cult,' (because that's what the media dubbed us). And yet Ti, who is my Father, who is my 'Older

Member,' who gave me birth in the Kingdom of Heaven long before this civilization began, Ti was here with me on this particular mission.

"Ti left, in Earth time 1985, because Ti had assisted enough that it was time to turn responsibility over to Do, and for me then to begin a more serious communication with my Older Member, and to be dependent upon it and reliant upon it."

Peep is dead, long live Ti.

After Peep's death, nothing much was heard from the UFO Cult until the early '90s. In 1993, the group reemerged with, a new urgency, an amended spiel and far more importantly, new technology.

The Do and Ti traveling UFO show went back on the road—in cyberspace, a brave new world of limitless borders, and no cops to patrol them.

It isn't known who may have initiated the elderly Do and his crew to the vast universe and possibilities of the Internet. Clearly, it was the only true outerspace Do would ever know.

For the missionary zealot that Do was first, last, and always, there could be no better place to preach and proselytize—and to make a good buck while you're at it!

There are about twenty-five million interactive visitors to the Internet in the United States, experts say. The network has long been a research tool—a link for scholars and students to a vast store of information, and each other.

But in the '90s, it also became a popular way to talk to people with similar interests, no matter how unusual, how bizarre. How out there.

". . . [T]he assumption of anonymity is surely one of the lures of communicating via clicking keyboards and coolly lit screens," writer Daphne Merkin told *U.S. News & World Report* in 1996.

"It is increasingly clear that the twilight, mediated world of the Internet is a perfect breeding ground for victims looking to be victimized.

"Denuded of the human aspect and shielded by an impersonal atmosphere, how easy it is to invent yourself and to objectify another person."

Cyberspace is not just the American frontier, but the World Frontier. And there are villains wandering among the plain folk, with nary a lawman in site.

Even death stalks the Internet.

One of the earliest, eeriest and most heinous cases of cyberspace crime occurred on October 16, 1996, when a lonely house-wife from a suburb outside of Baltimore, Maryland, was strangled and buried behind the ramshackle trailer of her Internet pen-pal, who was charged with the murder.

On the Net, Sharon Lopatka, 35, was "nancy." Robert Glass, 45, a family man from Lenoir, North Carolina, was "slow-hand." Lurking behind the whimsical aliases were wild and dangerous electronic person-alities. These two explored them with grim enthusiasm, and finally, violent final-ity.

Investigators say Lopatka was a regular visitor to various bondage "chat rooms." But unlike others who passed in and out of such kinky chats, Lopatka was there for more than the thrill, the freedom, the sexual charge, the anonymity.

She was there to find someone to kill her.

"Want to talk about torturing to death?" one message posted on August 22 to a "chat room" dealing with necrophilia inquired, according to the *Washington Post*.

"I have kind of a fascination with torturing till death. . . . Of course, I can't speak about it with my family."

Fellow Net users claimed to have corresponded with the sender, who revealed herself to be Lopatka.

"She was going into chat rooms and asking to be tortured to death, for real," Tanith Tyrr told the newspaper.

Not many played along with the e-mail fantasy for long. But Glass exchanged messages with Lopatka, allegedly describing in two e-mail missives exactly what kind of violence he would inflict on Lopatka. Court papers showed Lopatka left her home October 13, 1996, to meet Glass, apparently expecting to act out those descriptions of her death.

She told her husband she was headed to visit friends in Georgia for a week, police said. Much later, investigators would find this pathetic notice on her computer.

"If my body is never retrieved, don't worry. Know that I am at peace," the *Washington Post* reported.

Glass claimed the sex got out of hand, but that death was just an accident. The case has yet to come to trial.

Just a few months later after the Lopatka murder exploded onto the newspapers across the land, there was yet another murder case connected with the Internet.

Raymond Stumpf, 54, a late-night home-shopping host on a cable channel out of Pottstown, Pennsylvania, allegedly hacked his forty-seven-year-old wife to death on January 20, 1997—five days after a popular radio talk-show host from Philadelphia, Howard Eskin, sent the woman a dozen red roses.

Eskin told cops he'd been corresponding on the Internet with Stumpf, who used the cybername of "Brandis," for about a month before he decided to "brighten her day" and sent the poseys.

Along with the flowers, came a note: "Stay positive. You provoke a lot of interesting thought."

The husband, spotting the bouquet, flew into a rage and lunged at his wife with a knife, nearly severing her head. He then tried to kill himself. His case also is pending.

Those two murder cases may be the only ones linked to the Internet. Far more common Net crimes involve the deviates who stalk cyberspace.

The crimes differed; the allure was the same. Space, lots of space, to hide or metamorphize into whatever creature you could imagine.

"It's just that there's something about a medium where you can make yourself up as you go along," Doug Davis, a psychology professor at Haverford College told the *New York Post*.

The crimes don't all end in murder, but their occurrence—and frequency—is startling and disturbing enough.

Take these recent examples:

In November 1996, a thirty-year-old engineer from Yardley, Pennsylvania, was charged with traveling to Chicago to have sex with a thirteen-year-old girl he met on the Internet. That same month, a fifteen-year-old student was charged after he brought six ounces of homemade napalm to his Pennsylvania high school; he got the napalm recipe off the Net.

The list goes on:

A Pennsylvania man was arrested in October 1996 after getting caught in a police sting where he allegedly sought sex with a twelve-year-old boy through the Internet.

The same month, a man was arrested in Florida when he went to a gas station expecting to meet and have sex with a thirteen-year-old girl with whom he had conversed on the Internet. The teen turned out to be the sheriff who heads the crimes-against-children unit.

In early 1995, a former University of Michigan student was charged after he sent rape and death fantasies through a computer network. A federal judge later quashed the indictment.

Later that same year, a teenaged boy from Long Island was charged with harassment after he allegedly sent threatening e-mail messages, including one in which he supposedly threatened to sodomize a twelve-year-old girl.

In December, 1995, a nineteen-year-old disabled woman was raped by a man she met on the Internet.

Whether on-line or off, it's the high-profile

cases that tended to get the most attention. So it was with one of the most shocking sex-on-the-Net cases, which erupted in New York City in December 1996, and involved members of the city's educational and cultural elite.

Columbia grad student Oliver Jovanovich was charged with a November 1996 sex attack and torture of a Barnard student with whom he'd struck up an e-mail relationship. The suspect's mother was a violinist for the New York City Ballet. His father, an esteemed chess coach at one of the best private schools in the city.

Even the mass killer once known as the most hated man in America got his own website.

"The Charles Manson Home Page" is run by loyal followers who post quotes, photos and information about the convicted killer on the Internet.

At his parole hearing on March 27, 1997 the sixty-two-year-old serial killer and ex-cult leader shocked prison officials by declaring he didn't want to leave prison because he was working on his Internet site.

The inmate at the maximum-security Corcoran State Prison near Sacramento, California, has no access to a computer, modem, or other equipment necessary to craft an Internet page.

Manson had better than that. Former cult members who love him.

Sandra Good and others have put together the "Access Manson" site, complete with photos of Manson, his favorite quotes, a description of his legal status and other items. The site also includes information about his music.

The fifty-two-year-old Good—who served a decade in jail for sending threatening letters to businessmen—lives near the prison and was a member of the Manson Family.

What has grabbed the politicians' attention with far more urgency has been cybersmut, which some people have perceived as a persistent and troubling Internet menace for the past several years.

But it has taken almost two years for the issue to go all the way to the nation's high court to be resolved.

At issue is the 1996 Communications

Decency Act, which made it a crime to put indecent words or pictures online where children can find them.

"The Internet threatens to give every child a free pass into the equivalent of every adult bookstore and every adult video store in the country," Justice Department lawyer Seth Waxman told the Supreme Court in March 1997.

The subject is hotly debated. But it isn't expected to be decided by the Supreme Court of the United States until July of 1997.

For the time being, the cybercriminals roam free—or at least until they get caught up in a snare of their own making.

That was just the case of a Catholic priest in Britain, Father Adrian McLeish, who pleaded guilty in November 1996 to assaulting four young boys. McLeish used the Internet to boast about his crimes to other pedophiles. Police tracked him down after raiding the home of another pedophile and finding thirty-seven contact numbers.

In general, cops know they'll have to jump on line to catch the criminals lurking there.

"It's probably the wave of the future for law enforcement," the designer of one Michigan police force's Internet site told the *Detroit News* in the summer of 1996. "Forward-thinking people who can see beyond the immediate uses are what makes this so exciting."

The *Detroit News* reported five hundred U.S. police departments are online. So is the FBI, the nation's premier law enforcement agency, which posts its Ten Most Wanted list on the World Wide Web and has captured at least one dangerous criminal with a tip received from a Net surfer.

There may never be a child-proofed, sanitized Internet. By its very nature—and that of its users—it cannot be.

Online services have "allowed people total anonymity," one female user told the *Post and Courier* of Charleston, South Carolina in 1996. "Because of that anonymity, they feel a greater freedom to explore their darker side. They just feel totally liberated. It's almost as if there's no moral constraints on them anymore."

It's not just stalkers, sleaze and cultists polluting the Net.

Not by a long shot.

Bizarre screeds are part of the Internet landscape, as common as trees and grass along a ride in the country. Computer users generally find the weirdest Internet sideshows in the vast collection of Usenet discussion groups. But in reality, most people pass them right by without looking.

Bizarre groups just go with the territory.

Militia groups began using the Internet to recruit new members, sell propaganda, or cheerlead each other as far back as 1995.

"People who I thought would never go near computers are flocking to the Internet. It's definitely a priority in the militia movements," Brad Alpert, a computer programmer and member of the 51st Militia in Kansas City, Missouri told the *New York Post* in April 1995.

Instead of handing out leaflets in parking lots, a computer-armed militiaman can zap his message over the Net in a nano-second.

"It bypasses the traditional media and basically permits the rapid dissemination of useful information," Alpert told the newspaper.

Experts on such groups have warned that such uncensored cyberspace can also link isolated kooks with the movements that love them.

"Because you can send mass messages anonymously, you can do the equivalent of a drive-by hate attack without worrying about anybody reading your license plate," Rabbi Abraham Cooper of the Simon Wiesenthal Center said.

"It empowers these people. It gives them a sense of community and an unprecedented opportunity to disseminate their ideas."

After the April 1995 bombing of the federal building in Oklahoma City, the fringe militia groups knew their isolation was over.

"Hello ATF, FBI, NSA, CIA, etc. We know you're watching," one message off the Net noted shortly after the disaster.

"They are very paranoid people and the Oklahoma event has intensified their paranoia," Mark Pitcavage, a militia expert at Ohio State University, told the newspaper.

Like cybersmut, there are some community leaders who believe a little censorship would go a long way. But unplugging the message of hate groups has so far failed to win the hearts and minds of lawmakers.

"This is where it gets really rough, because emotionally it is so appealing," Esther Dyson, chairwoman of the Electronic Frontier Foundation, told the *New York Times* in 1996. "Yes, most of the stuff is despicable. But it is still censorship."

In fact, it is all too easy to find websites operated by neo-Nazis, skinheads and other racist groups.

"We correctly label these groups as lunatic fringe," Rabbi Cooper told the *New York Times* in 1996.

"But it is a mistake to think they lack sophistication. They have embraced this technology quicker than any other group of society. For them it is a technology made in heaven."

There are thirty to forty million web pages on the Internet, calculates Karen Coyle of Computer Users for Social Responsibility—certainly plenty of space for a UFO-crazy cult to log in.

Welcome aboard, UFOlogists!

In 1993, under the name Total Overcomers Anonymous, Do's refigured crew, with its recycled message, took out a full-page ad in *USA Today*, proclaiming: "UFO Cult Resurfaces with Final Offer."

According to Robert Balch, the ad "focused primarily on the group's beliefs, which appeared to have changed little in the last eighteen years. However, it had an apocalyptic tone that was much more dramatic than anything I had heard in 1975.

"The earth's present 'civilization' is about to be recycled—'spaded under.' Its inhabitants are refusing to evolve. The 'weeds' have taken over the garden and disturbed its usefulness beyond repair."

There were sporadic new sitings of the new crew—usually without the aging eunuch Do.

"One night this week, forty inquiring souls entered a University of Illinois at Chicago classroom; a flier outside the room billed the lecture/discussion as 'UFOs, Space Aliens and Their Final Fight for Earth's Spoils,'" the *Chicago Tribune* reported on July 29, 1994.

"Curiosity brought that audience face-to-face with the remnants of a nomadic community that aroused the media and law enforcement in the 1970s . . . as members appeared at three Chicago-area locations this week, one of their fliers declared: 'We're back.'"

The new disciples spewed anew the mantra of Bo and Peep: Abandon your old self, disregard the "vessel" of your body and all forms of sexuality, relationships and addictions. Doing so will be "one of the hardest things you'll ever do," one of the disciples reportedly told the small crowd. But it'll be worth it—you'll eventually win a ride on a spaceship that will take you to the heavens.

The group seemed harmless enough in its revitalized form—even according to Balch, who knew them all too well.

"I don't think this is a dangerous cult," he told the *Tribune.* "It is not in the mold of the Charles Manson family, Jim Jones' Peoples Temple or David Koresh's Branch Davidians. It does not have a violent history. But it can be dangerous from a parents' perspective. Anybody who joins this group is going to drop out of sight."

There were other stops along the recruitment trail in 1994: a meeting in Taos, New Mexico in April of that year; another later gathering in Madison, Wisconsin.

Another cult expert, Bob Waldrep, told the *New York Times* he ran into the resurfaced group in Birmingham, Alabama. That meeting ran three hours, during which time disciples referred to Older Members who, peculiarly, were more into earthly dieting than heavenly repose.

"The O.M.s have experimented with many different diets for us to determine the most efficient," Waldrep recalled the group members saying, the *New York Times* reported. "The only purpose for food is to fuel the vehicles."

Vehicles was Heaven's Gate–speak for bodies.

That year seemed to be the very last for public addresses by the group. From 1995 on, the cult would expand its reach as far as modern technology could take it, as far as the Internet would allow.

In 1995, the core group was reported moving around northern San Diego County in California, renting big houses, dressing in black shirts and pants, holding garage sales where buyers found high-tech, expensive electronic equipment at rock-bottom prices.

Around that time as well—the exact start is not known—Heaven's Gate went into business, as Higher Source, a computer programming firm that would earn a small but enthusiastic reputation among San Diego County business clients.

On the Net, Higher Source had a conventional website at which the business offered design services, Internet security services, computer programming, computer network services, and digital telephone work.

"The individuals at the core of our group have worked closely together for over twenty years," Higher Source touted to cyberspace shoppers.

"During those years, each of us has developed a high degree of skill and know-how through personal discipline and concerted effort. We try to stay positive in every circumstance and put the good of a project above any personal concerns or artistic egos. By sustaining this attitude and conduct, we have achieved a high level of efficiency and quality in our work. This crew-minded effort, combined with ingenuity and creativity, have helped us provide advanced solutions at highly competitive rates."

To all appearances, Higher Source was hawking its wares in the most modern and marketing savvy way possible. For all the world, the confident sassy-sounding crew could have been the next pretender to the computer world crown.

"We at Higher Source not only cater to customizing websites that will enhance your company image, but strive to make your transition into the 'world of cyberspace' a very easy and fascinating experience."

Beverly Hills businessman Nick Matzorkis was one of the clients serviced by the Higher Source "crew." Its workers were weird, he acknowledged—dressing identically and calling themselves monks. But their work was superb.

By 1996, Heaven's Gate had a website of its own as well. But this home page was anything but staid.

On the Heaven's Gate home page, there were offerings both mystical and mystifying: "Our Position Against Suicide," "Last Chance to Advance Beyond Human," "How a Member of the Kingdom of Heaven Might Appear," "Statement by a Crewmember," "'95 Statement by An E.T. Presently Incarnate," "Do's Intro: Purpose-Belief," "Last Chance to Evacuate Earth."

The home page was a treasure trove of Applewhite's and Nettles's philosophy, updated, refined, and perfectly packaged for an insane Age of Computers.

Some of it read like a cross between a children's fairy tale, the script from the television movie science-fiction thriller made about Applewhite and Nettles, a compilation of the best of *Star Trek*—and the hallucinations of a paranoid schizophrenic.

Once upon a time . . .

"In the early 1970s, two individuals (my task partner and myself) from the Evolutionary Level Above Human (the Kingdom of Heaven) incarnated into (moved into and took over) two human bodies that were in their forties. I moved into a male body, and my partner, who is an Older Member in the Level Above Human, took a female body. (We called these bodies 'vehicles,' for they simply served as physical vehicular tools for us to wear while on a task among humans. They had been tagged and set aside for our use since their birth.)" read an entry titled "'95 Statement by an E.T. Presently Incarnate," and written by Do.

"We brought to Earth with us a crew of students whom we had worked with (nurtured) on Earth in previous missions. They were in varying stages of metamorphic transition from membership in the human kingdom to membership in the physical Evolutionary Level Above Human (what your history refers to as the Kingdom of God or Kingdom of Heaven).

"It seems that we arrived in Earth's atmosphere between Earth's 1940s and early 1990s. We suspect that many of us arrived in staged spacecraft (UFO) crashes and many of our discarded bodies (genderless, not belonging to the human species), were retrieved by human authorities (government and military).

"Other crews from the Level Above Human preceded our arrival and 'tagged'—placed a despite 'chip'—in each of the vehicles (bodies) that we would individually incarnate into, when that instruction would be given. These 'chips' set aside those bodies for us.

"We feel that while we were 'out of body' between arrival and incarnation, we were thoroughly briefed and were taken through

an extensive preview of places and events
that would assist our individual incarnation
process of bringing out our mind—our con-
sciousness—into the vehicle (body) and
overriding the mind of the human 'plant'
(or container) that each of us was to use.

"This incarnation process is very difficult
and cannot be done without the help of
Older Members of the Evolutionary Level
Above Human who have not only gone
through the metamorphic transition to
completion themselves, but who have also
assisted others through this transition
before (acting as 'midwives' for some in the
shedding of their human-creature characteristics while preparing to be born as new
creatures into the Next Evolutionary
Kingdom.). . ."

It was almost laughable in its arcane
detail, its obsessive meticulousness, it bone-
dry preachiness.

There was a prescription for every ill, an
answer for every question. None of it made
much practical sense.

The metamorphic "birth" into the Level
Above Human occurs as follows, Do
explained:

"In any given civilization on a fertile planet such as Earth (and Earth has had many periodic/cyclical civilizations), the Level Above Human plants all the new life forms (including humans) for that civilization in a neutral condition so that they have a chance to choose the direction of their growth. The Level Above Human—or Next Level—directly (hands on) relates significantly to the civilization at its beginning stage, and subsequently (with few exceptions) at approximately 2000-year intervals (48-hour intervals from a Next Level perspective) until that civilization's final 'Age.'

"Each time the Next Level relates directly to any portion of that civilization, 'deposits' containing 'souls' (the 'seed' or 'chip' with a program of metamorphic possibilities) are placed in many human plants. This deposit is potentially the 'fight of life' into the physical and real Evolutionary Level Above Human. These deposits are given or made only when members of the Level Above Human are assigned to directly relate to (be incarnate in) the civilization. Only these Representatives can 'nurture' those deposited souls with Next Level thinking, behavior, and all the information required to effectively 'fluff off' all human/mammalian characteristics of the old creature. (A potential creature of the Next Level cannot cling to human ways any more than a butterfly can cling to caterpillar ways.) So, when a Representative from that Kingdom is present—that 'Rep's' nurturing (teaching) is a 'window' for exiting the human kingdom for all who have been given deposits/souls. These deposits are made only in vehicles (bodies) that are 'old enough'— having grown or matured enough—for self-determination or responsibility."

The cult had forsaken most of its earlier spirituality. By 1995, it was rewriting biology.

"Humans in any given time seem to fall in one of three categories," the same cyberspace "statement" contended.

"Humans without deposits—those who are simply 'plants' (a part of the various levels of human 'plant' life) containing the mind or program of their genetic information combined with their brain's interpretation of the information of their current body's experiences, those with deposits/souls who are receiving nourishment from the present Rep(s) toward metamorphic completion, and those with deposits/souls who are not in a classroom nor in a direct relationship with the Representative(s) from the Level Beyond Human, having not been confronted with the information and the Rep(s) or been confronted but have chosen to 'pursue.'"

What religion remained in the cult's philosophy was juiced up to *Star Trek* banality. The cult's statement contends anyone who isn't for them, is surely against them—and evil to boot.

"Those with souls—who fall away—become a part of the opposition to the Next Level. Once, in a prior civilization, records suggest that a third of the class fell and the strongest and thereby leader of those fallen, was called 'Lucifer' (or Satan). Even today they occupy the near heavens as what humans refer to as 'space aliens.' They also burrow in bases underground and participate in genetic manipulation and hybridization with humans, and attempt to recruit (while remaining among the 'unseen') those humans with souls who are unstable or weak in their pursuit of the true Kingdom of Heaven.

"These 'luciferians' (for the most part from the 'unseen' world) started all religions and masquerade as 'gods' to humans. They offer to humans (who are unknowingly praying to them) whatever material gains they desire. These 'Luciferians' and their devotees preach life in the human condition, and are determined to take the steps to make the inhabitants of the plane subservient to their 'ideal' mammalian ethic—destructive to the natural evolutionary processes, and abhorrent to the Kingdom Level Above Human . . ."

The foreboding in that statement was anything but subtle, and surprisingly soothing.

"Since this is the close of the Age, the battle in the Heavens with their servants on Earth will be the means of that closing and the spading under of the plants (including humans) of this civilization. 'Weeds' are now getting rid of weeds—from gang wars to nations involved in ethnic cleansing. This is simply a part of the natural recycling process which precedes a restoration period of the planet in preparation for another civilization's beginning."

It's impossible to say what kind of effect the cyberspace ramblings had on recruitment; clearly, Higher Source caught some business.

But what kind of effect could the Heaven's Gate home page have on recruiting new travelers for that future spaceship ride to the stars?

One Heaven's Gate member's "Statement by a Crewmember" reflected not only how slavishly devoted "Tddody" was to Do and Ti, how ready "Tddody" was to die.

It also showed that, just perhaps, the rejiggered cult coming out of hiding and onto the Internet may have pulled back a lost soul who wandered from the flock.

The crewmember calculated he first met Bo and Peep around 1978, dropped out three years later, and then dropped back in around 1994.

It was a startling view of the cult from someone who professed to have been there at the start:

"My only objective here is to reflect my feelings and state of mind at the time of my exit from the mainstream world . . .

". . . I first came in contact with Ti and Do

(my Teachers) in the mid '70s at a meeting in California. At that meeting, things occurred that in no way could be called coincidence. As Do spoke, questions would come to mind, as I would think the question, Do would say something like, 'Some may wonder about' and state the question I was thinking. When this occurred, I felt as if I were in a tunnel with Do at one end and me at the other. Although I sat in the back of a packed auditorium, it was as if no one else were there, but He (Do) and His Older Member (Ti) and myself.

"Although I didn't immediately enter the classroom, a couple of months had passed when I remembered Do saying something like, 'If you're seeking the Truth, this message is what you're going to find,' and something like, 'Go into the closet of your mind and ask to the Highest Source you can.' The day I actually did this, I came in contact with this information again. At that first meeting with Ti and Do, I somehow knew they were who they said they were— Representatives (Reps) from the Kingdom of Heaven.

"I admit to having had feelings of fear,

but I knew I had to respond. Everything they said made perfect sense. They didn't solicit new members and told of the requirements about what it took to get to the Next Level—total commitment and total energy. And those who couldn't stick to the discipline were encouraged to leave. I was in the class for three years, working at freeing myself of all the human ties and addictions that would bind me to this planet, when I was sent out of the classroom. I didn't know why I was being sent out, and for a time wondered if I'd been abandoned. I never forgot Ti and Do for the fifteen years (or more) I was out of the class. The entire time, I am aware now, the Next Level monitored and guided me through a series of tests and growth experiences I feel that I would have never gained had I been in the classroom.

"The entire time out there (in the world) I learned about human love, and how shallow it really is, how it turns to hate and mistrust and deceit in a moment, and that all endeavors out there at best are self-serving, self-indulgent, shallow victories and usually come at the expense of someone else's toil or pain. Many of the leaders of this country (as well as other countries) are liars, hypocrites, and deceitful scam artists that seem to have no more comprehension of Truth than a box of rocks. The government is so corrupt and has run renegade and is not very different from Genghis Khan, Attila the Hun, or Hitler . . .

"While in this world, I had tasted success and found it to be very rude, mean, aggressive, and quite abrasive and distasteful—'qualities' I have no wish to enhance or develop. I have seen the world through a thousand pairs of eyes and despised it each and every time—without exception!

"The only true happiness I'd ever really know was when I was with my teachers—Ti and Do. In October of 1994, I was guided by the grace of the Next Level into a 'chance meeting' with my former classmates, and I expressed my sincere and earnest desire to re-enter the class. I wanted to finish the task I started eighteen years ago, the task of totally overcoming the world and freeing myself of addictions and sensuality and all the human traps of this world. My classmates are the only other ones on this planet that understand me and what I've been through, as I understand them and know what they've gone through . . .

"I am healthier, happier, and in a better frame of mind than I have ever been in. I'm eager to take up my life in a body belonging to the Next Level . . ."

By September 29, 1996, Do's Internet tirades took on an ominous tone—much more so than usual.

Perhaps he was ill; he sounded so.

"Truth. I want to leave here. Now," he wrote in the message titled "Last Chance to Evacuate Earth Before It's Recycled.

"I'm in a vehicle that is already falling apart on me, and I'm desperate to try to help you have a last chance to go. . . . I don't mean to make fun of this. I am desperate—for your sakes. Within the past twenty-four hours I have been clearly informed by my Older Member of how short the remaining time is; how clearly we cannot concentrate on anything except the perspective that says: the end of this civilization is very close. The end of a civilization is accompanied by spading under, refurbishing the planet in preparation for

another civilization. And the only ones who
can survive that experience have to be
those who are taken into the keeping of the
Evolutionary Level Above Human."

In the message, Do also talked about
what the cult had been doing before its
foray onto the Net.

"We put out a statement called '88
Update' and we did a videotape series a little while after that, I think it was 1992,
called 'Beyond Human.'"

It wasn't work Do wanted to talk about.
The lecture was vintage Bo, only updated to
be environmentally correct as well as spiritually on target.

"Our reason for speaking to you is
because we feel (sic) to warn you of what is
just around the corner.

"I'll try to just put it as briefly as I can and
as clearly as I can. This planet is about to be
recycled, refurbished, started over. That
doesn't mean it's going to be destroyed, it
doesn't mean it's the end of the world. But
it does mean that it is going to be spaded
under. . . ."

Then, perhaps in a nod to his long-gone
soulmate, Peep, Do went on a rambling dis-

course that combined a fanciful reincarnation theory with a revised version of the Christian standby, the fall of the bad angel, Lucifer.

"A long time ago, long before this civilization began (and I don't know how many subsequent times this occurred), that Kingdom Level had a Representative in a human civilization, and members of a classroom who were in the process of overcoming their human characteristics. Some of those members who began to serve in elementary ways for that Kingdom Level Above Human decided that they didn't want to listen to that Representative any more, that they could do the things they wanted to do, and they weren't sure they wanted to get rid of human ways. And so they began to find fault in the Representative who was offering them a way out of the human kingdom. Well, you know the story from there—fallen angels, Lucifer, Satan, a third of the Heavens following a renegade who decided, 'This world is not for me. I can be my own "god." I don't need that Kingdom Level. I resent that I cannot be my own individual—that I can't lead my own flock.'

"Well, that Kingdom Level Above Human let that individual and his following lead their flock—let them do what they wanted to do—and used it for means that could serve a purpose in the design of the Next Level progression. And that very evil presence is thick on this planet because it's the End of an Age. It's so thick that it would have you not believe a world I say, and have you not accept anything that I tell you so that you will not be a recipient of the Kingdom they left (that they got booted out of and want no one else to go there). They are resentful—and are in opposition to the real Kingdom Level Above Human. . . ."

Do tried to explain how he "arrived" on this planet. It was a bit of whimsy not lost on the crazy old man.

"When Ti and I were awakening, we entered this environment (to any significant degree) in the early '70s. You're looking at the body I'm wearing and you're saying, 'You entered in the early '70s? You're certainly more than twenty-something years old.' The body I'm wearing is, WOW! Sixty-five years old. 'I' (the mind/soul of the Next Level) entered at the same time my Older

Member entered, which was in the early '70s. You could think, 'Well, that doesn't make any sense.' If you're 'New Age'—or whatever your belief is regarding reincarnation—you could think, 'Well, I don't understand, I thought reincarnation occurs at the beginning of an infant's life.' No, I'm sorry to say, that's not accurate.

"A mind begins when that infant is born, and that infant's genetic package begins to express itself as that mind develops. And it is a mind, it is a spirit. But then a spirit or a mind that had previously occupied another human plant, but has gone into the spirit world (or is outside of a body because it lost its body from death or whatever, but is still in the environment), can move in and take over that vehicle and be stronger than the mind that is the mind of that vehicle.

"In other worlds, it can invade that vehicle. It can take it over. It can pretty much keep the mind of that vehicle quiet and do what it wants to do with that vehicle . . .

"When Ti and I were brought into this environment in the early '70s, a spacecraft brought us in—remember, it's a physical world. And actually we came in earlier and made deposits, or little 'information deposits,' in our vehicles when they were infants. So, that means we had to come in during the late '20s and early '30s. We also had to come in and make deposits in the vehicles of all the classroom that are sitting here in front of me at the various times when those vehicles were infants."

It was the last gasp of the desperate old cult leader—an explanation for the years of wandering and waiting.

But there was still the nagging question.

When would the spaceship come that was supposed to whisk them to the heavens above, the level-above-human?

At that time, Do said he didn't know yet the end for which he so urgently warned, and so earnestly longed.

"How is this end of civilization going to occur?" he asks, answering his own question with the one that frustrated followers for twenty-one years.

"I don't know all the particulars."

Suicide wasn't an option, the group proclaimed. But of course, it was doublespeak in the best tradition of Heaven's Gate-speak. Reading "Our Position Against Suicide" reveals the group was all too ready to take the final step.

Still in all, Do seemed just as worried about an FBI raid on his compound, much in the same way the FBI stormed Waco and Ruby Ridge.

"We know that it is only while we are in these physical vehicles (bodies) that we can learn the lessons needed to complete our own individual transition, as well as to complete our task of offering the Kingdom of Heaven to this civilization one last time. We take good care of our vehicles so they can function well for us in this task, and we try to protect them from any harm.

"We fully desire, expect, and look forward to boarding a spacecraft from the Next Level very soon (in our physical bodies). There is no doubt in our mind that our being 'picked up' is inevitable in the very near future. But what happens between now and then is the big question. We are keenly aware of several possibilities.

"It could happen that before that spacecraft comes, one or more of us could lose our physical vehicles (bodies) due to 'recall,' accident, or at the hands of some irate individual. We do not anticipate this, but it is possible. Another possibility is that, because of the position we take in our information, we could find so much disfavor with the powers that control this world that there could be attempts to incarcerate us or to subject us to some sort of psychological or physical torture (such as occurred at both Ruby Ridge and Waco.)

"It has always been our way to examine all possibilities, and be mentally prepared for whatever may come our way. For example, consider what happened at Masada around 73 A.D. A devout Jewish sect, after holding out against a siege by the Romans to the best of their ability, and seeing that the murder, rape, and torture of their community was inevitable, determined that it was permissible for them to evacuate their bodies by a more dignified, and less agonizing method. We have thoroughly discussed this topic (of willful exit of the body under such conditions), and have mentally prepared ourselves for this possibility (as can be seen in a few of our statements). However, this act certainly does not need serious consideration at this time, and hopefully will not in the future.

"The true meaning of 'suicide' is to turn against the Next Level when it is being offered. In these last days, we are focused on two primary tasks: one—of making a last attempt at telling the truth about how the Next Level may be entered (our last effort at offering to individuals of this civilization the way to avoid 'suicide'); and two—taking individually on our personal overcoming and change, in preparation for entering the Kingdom of Heaven."

Do and his followers had moved into the sprawling mansion at Rancho Santa Fe in San Diego County in October 1996.

Just prior to that, they had lived about fifty-five miles southeast of Albuquerque, New Mexico, in an isolated compound with a wall of tires they dubbed their "Earth Ship."

The cult abandoned the compound last year, leaving behind much of their equipment.

Jim Thorsen, who bought the property from cult members, said the place was partly surrounded by walls of dirt-filled tires as high as twenty feet. The tire walls were part of the plans for an "Earth Ship" culled from a book called "Earth Ship, How to Build Your Own," Thorsen said.

Thorsen said cult members did not tell him why they were selling the land or where they were going, and left behind bunk beds, power tools and portable generators. They lived in a metal-walled, factory-like building, in cabins dotting the property and in two sixty-square-foot tents.

Thorsen said they had planned to build an infirmary, a nursery, a bakery, a pharmacy and workshops.

Things changed quickly.

With the move into the swanky Rancho Santa Fe mansion, the rag-tag cultists evolved into a demented monastery. The even referred to one another as monks.

There was reportedly an obsession with food and order.

The members ate one big communal meal at 5:00 A.M., published reports said, and no other meals. Instead, hungry members could snack on fruit and a lemon drink seasoned with cayenne pepper.

Wake-up and prayer was reportedly conducted each day at 3:00 A.M.

They loved *Star Trek* and *The X-Files*.

Non-cult members were not welcomed, and did not come. Those that came were too frightened to stick around.

"I was too afraid to even walk toward the house," pool cleaner Lawrence Jimenez told a tabloid TV show.

Jimenez got nothing but icy reserve from cult members in mid March 1997 when he went to clean the pool behind the mansion/headquarters for the cult.

The cult members, in their regular black garb, trained a telescope on him and asked each other, "Do we have him?" he said. "The whole time I was out there my hands were shaking and I was practically in tears."

On March 24, Jimenez said he was jolted when he overhead several cult members talking about something that was to happen March 26 or March 27. Something ominous.

"I said to myself what have these guys got planned? I felt more and more uneasy. There were just all sorts of cars, expensive cars, brand new Cadillacs, real big motor home–type things you can carry twenty people in. There were New Mexico license plates and quite a few of them had Texas plates.

"I was totally intimidated because of their mannerisms. Every time I thought of them, I thought of Guyana. It just gave me that sort of aura the whole time."

What significant event was Do flock's discussing in urgent whispers that March 24?

It may have been what many other people across the nation were talking and thinking about. For once, Do and his followers were looking skyward at exactly the same time as the rest of America.

Except the comet racing through the sky was far more to Do than "the big dirty snowball" its discoverer described it to be.

For this newly discovered Hale-Bopp comet—and a rumor swirling around it— was the opening Heaven's Gate had been hoping, praying, and expecting to slip through on a spaceship to the beyond.

Hale-Bopp was discovered July 23, 1995, when Alan Hale and Thomas Bopp, located a fuzzy spot in the constellation Sagittarius, some 500 million miles away.

The International Astronomical Union quickly confirmed the existence of the comet, and named it after the two men. The comet in late March and early April of 1997 got the closest it will come to Earth, still 100 million miles away.

In November 1996, another amateur astronomer gave the cult the phony news it had been waiting for.

The Houston stargazer claimed on the Internet and a radio talk show to have sighted a mysterious craft behind the comet.

The long-awaited starship!

Though reputable astronomers jumped all over the UFO theory—proving it was just a star distorted by the optics of a telescope—Do and his followers had their "marker."

The end was very near.

"Red Alert. HALE-BOPP Brings Closure," Heaven's Gate blared on the Internet.

"Whether Hale-Bopp has a 'companion' or not is irrelevant from our perspective. However, its arrival is joyously very significant to us at 'Heaven's Gate.' The joy is that our Older Member in the Evolutionary Level Above Human (the 'Kingdom of Heaven') has made it clear to us that Hale-Bopp's approach is the 'marker' we've been waiting for—the time for the arrival of the spacecraft from the Level Above Human to take us home to 'Their World'—in the Literal Heavens. Our twenty-two years of classroom here on planet Earth is finally coming to conclusion—'graduation' from the Human Evolutionary Level. We are happily prepared to leave 'this world' and go with Ti's crew.

"If you study the material on this website you will hopefully understand our joy and what our purpose here on Earth has been. You may even find your 'boarding pass' to leave with us during this brief 'window.'

"We are so very thankful that we have been recipients of this opportunity to prepare for membership in Their Kingdom, and to experience Their boundless Caring and Nurturing."

Do and his followers soon abandoned cyberspace for a shot at outerspace.

Their bags packed, a lethal drug cocktail recipe prepared, their rooms neat, their past abandoned, their futures secured, Do and thirty-eight followers prepared to board the long-delayed flight to the Heavenly Kingdom.

But they didn't say their farewells on the Internet.

Their apologies were offered on videotape.

"I look very, very forward to this next major step of ours where we're going to be shedding these creatures, these primitive creatures that we have used for our lesson ground and that we're going to be moving on to the next evolutionary level above human," said the skinny youth's partner on the videotape segment, a bespectacled middle-aged man in a plaid shirt buttoned up to the neck.

"I think everyone in this class wanted something more than this human world had to offer," said one woman all in black and close-cropped brown hair.

"We're looking forward to this. We're happy and excited," smiled one buck-toothed woman with similarly close cropped hair and glasses.

"You know, these are like vehicles. I mean if you use the analogy of a car and, you know, people may keep their cars for a long time before they finally wear out and conk out and they die on 'em and, you know, they go and get another car. . . . I mean that's all we're talking about. It's not a big deal," insisted a young-looking man in an open-at-the collar black shirt.

"By the time you read this, we suspect that the human bodies we were wearing have been found, and that a flurry of fragmented reports have begun to hit the wire services," a letter sent to a former cult member explained.

"We'll be gone—several dozen of us. We came from the Level Above Human in distant space and we have now exited the bodies that we were wearing for our earthly task, to return to the world from whence we came—task completed."

The die was cast.

It was now shortly after 3:30 in the afternoon of March 26. The world was about to find out about Bo and Peep and their wacky cult of death.

Chapter

7

THE TRUE BELIEVERS

There is one true thing about the thirty-eight people who followed an aging, raging eunuch to their deaths inside a three million California mansion: Each took the mad, hopeless gamble on mortality with serene, joyous determination.

What would make them turn their backs on family, friends, and the future—shunning normal, productive, even envious lives? What convinced them a crazy old man held their tickets to eternity aboard a starship from heaven?

The videotaped farewells of some of the thirty-eight victims of Heaven Gate's mass suicide poignantly proved just how easy it was for those lost souls, so desperately sick at heart and so miserably consumed with despair to risk a suicide.

The families and friends of the other victims also gave important clues as to why the horrific tragedy occurred to a group perceived as so peaceful and gentle.

Sure they'd risk complicated lives for a simple one-way ride behind a comet. What else was there to lose?

• Bo and Peep's thirty-eight followers had already given up their lives the day they followed the mercurial pair of Texans.

"I think everyone in this class wanted something more than this human world had to offer," one of the cult members said in her good-bye videotape.

More? More of what, their families wanted to know.

They all had so much—families who loved them, children who missed them, friends who wondered about them.

Nowhere was the mystery, the *why* of their suicides, more disquietingly revealed than in the case of Yvonne McCurdy-Hill of Cincinnati, who moved into the cult's mansion only six months before she died.

To take that fateful, doomed step, the thirty-nine-year-old mother of five had turned her back on five kids, including twin girls born August 9, 1996—and named after the cult leaders, DoRae Mishelle and TeJa Lishelle. She and husband Steven Hill walked effortlessly away from jobs, family and friends in September 1996.

The couple were recruited to the aging shepherd and his flock through the Internet. He was a sci-fi freak, into *The X-Files*; she was a computer whiz.

They'd found kindred spirits in Heaven's Gate. More importantly, they both found a way to escape a difficult, burdened, and worrisome life.

Still, to Yvonne's family, there seemed no hint at all of turmoil, trouble, or discontent.

"She didn't show any signs, and that's why it's so shocking," Roger Reynolds, her childhood friend said. "Everybody knew her as the way she was here, not the way they found her."

"The way she was" was a gifted, devoted, and loving daughter growing up in a rowdy but solid family of six boys and two girls. Her father, Leroy McCurdy, who worked for the Postal Service for twenty-five years, and only sister, Lishell, were everything to her.

In May 1995, Yvonne's father died at age eighty, and things began to change.

With two boys under the age of five, Yvonne learned she was pregnant with twins. There were money problems. Yvonne had worked at the Postal Service for eleven years; her husband was a computer operator for Formica, a nearby factory. They were hounded by debt.

According to the *Cincinnati Enquirer*, two foreclosures were filed against Yvonne in the 1990s. First, in 1991, Fireman's Fund Morgage Corporation filed a foreclosure against her and her husband. Yvonne was listed as living in Wyoming at the time, and the action was dismissed in July 1991.

Another foreclosure started in December 1996. Provident Bank filed the action against her and Steven. Efforts to find the pair between January and March were unsuccessful, the court papers showed.

First, just Steven was going to ditch this harried life for a spurious, but simple, mission with the flying saucer and cybercult at Rancho Santa Fe, California. But Yvonne, just three weeks after the birth of the twins, would not be abandoned. She insisted on leaving, too.

Their families tried to persuade them to stay and got counselors for them. They even tried calling in the FBI.

"The FBI said they don't get involved in these things since Waco," Eartha Hill, Steven's mother, told the Associated Press. "The mental health people said when someone is this entrenched in a cult, it's too late."

Yvonne's co-workers at the Postal Service in Cincinnati also tried to talk her out of her decision, as did Steven's bosses at Formica.

They quit anyway, with Yvonne posting a simple notice at work, citing "circumstances beyond my control," the *Washington Post* reported.

"I said 'Where's the spaceship? I want to see it,' " Eartha Hill told the AP. "I said 'Boy, don't you know if there was a spaceship, you'd be the last one to get on that thing? They'd shoot it out of the sky.'"

Finally, those who loved Yvonne and Steven simply recoiled in horror at their departure.

When they arrived at Bo's front door,

they were assigned separate rooms and chaperones when together. Steven rejected voluntary castration.

"They understood they had to be celibate, but with the natural feeling between husband and wife I don't know if it went down that way," Eartha Hill told the *Washington Post*.

They worked, with Steven doing some of the writing for the website maintained by both the cult's business arm, The Higher Source, and its recruitment home page named Heaven's Gate. But, his mother said, he hated the relentless routine, the rigid regimentation.

He wanted to leave. He thought Yvonne did, too.

"They sent him on an errand and he went out, I think it was about an hour," Steven's mother told the newspaper. "When he got back, 'Do' was in the room with her and she had changed her mind. His heart was heavy. He had to leave her.

"'I tried mama, to get her out. I tried to get her out.'"

Steven, given a ticket back to Cincinnati instead of aboard a nonexistent spaceship, kept in contact with the cult via e-mail, but apparently had no idea what was soon to happen.

"It's my children's mother," he sobbed to his mother when he learned Yvonne committed suicide with other cult members.

"We got towels, we're crying so much," Eartha Hill said. "He tried everything to get his wife out of there, but they blocked him."

The same helpless outrage at a self-made jail in which their loved ones so happily lived and so willingly died has ripped apart each of the families of cult members.

Their stories, so different in details, were heartbreakingly similar in their emotion, their sheer devastation, their incredible loss.

LaDonna Brugato's family said they were "within a week" of reclaiming the forty-year-old violinist and computer programmer who had joined the Heaven's Gate cult in 1994.

They thought she had abandoned everything for God.

Still, the large Brugato family never quite understood the abrupt break with what to all appearances was a quiet, comfortable life in Newberg, Oregon, a college town of

14,000 people nestled in the lush greenery of the Pacific Northwest.

They never accepted it either.

"I did everything to find her," her devastated father, Joe Brugato, told reporters who crowded outside the family's home in search of an explanation for her membership in the comet-crazy cult, and her suicide with them.

"I personally and my family have been searching for her for three years, but always seemed to be one step behind her."

Brugato, a real-estate agent, said he became so desperate for any kind of information on his long-lost daughter that he finally resorted to hiring private investigator Gary Crowe.

"She told them she was in a traveling ministry and devoting her life to God," Crowe told the Associated Press. "There was no talk of UFOs . . . Hale-Bopp or anything like that."

Crowe finally hit paydirt in the winter of 1997. He doggedly tracked her down to a private mailbox company in La Jolla, California—a mere ten miles from Rancho Santa Fe.

So near, and yet so far away.

"We were within a week of getting her," Brugato said.

LaDonna Brugato, one of nine kids raised in a large, boisterous but comfortable home, was one of the computer whizzes recruited by Heaven's Gate who helped launch the UFO cult into cyberspace—and gave it a thriving computer programming business to boot.

The bright, nerdy LaDonna had been working as a computer programmer in Colorado when she dropped out of the real world, and into the wacky world of Marshall Herff Applewhite and his band of flying saucer freaks.

When investigators found her body—clad in black pants, black shirt, and black sneakers, and her hair shorn short, exactly like that of the other androgynous suicide victims—she carried a license in her pocket showing an address in Englewood, Colorado.

"She joined the cult . . . at a very vulnerable time in her life," her dad said. "She gave us little information about the group she had joined, or exactly what she was doing."

There'd been just two letters over two

excruciating years, LaDonna's father said. And neither hinted at the demented cult leader and his band of sexless, castrated followers.

Never was there the mention of a cult, or its weird-sounding philosophy posted all over the Internet.

LaDonna's family and her former friends had no idea her life had been totally based on a vain, silly hope for a free ride on a flying saucer.

"We received only two letters from her over the past two years in which she described her new life as a traveling minister," her father said. "She emphasized she was very happy with God."

LaDonna shielded her family and friends from her inner turmoil, but there were clear hints to others who knew her in Colorado.

There, the quiet, smart violinist seemed quite mystical, and open to anything that could provide explanations for the unexplainable, answers for the unknowable.

"She had a canopy bed set up with four diamond-shape crystals on each corner of her bed and one large crystal" suspended from the ceiling over the middle of her bed, one of LaDonna's former landlords in Colorado told the Associated Press.

"It clearly left me with the impression that this was some New Age experimental worship place that she used to commune with her gods."

To the world, LaDonna Brugato was just one more of the weirdo UFO cult, one of the space cadets who worked on computers and loved science fiction.

Her family never knew that woman.

"Donna was an intelligent, kind, and generous person. She was a gifted violinist and a talented computer programmer."

That's the mass suicide victim the Brugato family mourns.

When the horror of the carnage inside Rancho Sante Fe was revealed to the world, hundreds of families with missing family members held their breaths in hope—and horror.

Would their missing son, daughter, father, mother, wife, husband, be among the victims?

They wanted both to know, and to not know.

These were the painful emotions going

through Nancie Brown's mind when the San
Diego coroner called her on March 27, 1997.

For twenty-one years, Brown had no
idea where her son, David Geoffrey Moore,
had disappeared. But she wasn't surprised
at his death, or his devotion to the Heaven's
Gate cult, either.

Brown was aware of her son's bizarre
beliefs. She didn't fear them. There's a lot of
funny ideas in the world. Her son's beliefs
were at least peaceful. He didn't believe in
violence, she said.

"They valued a person's life," Brown told
the *Washington Post*. "But they also said they
felt that at some higher level they would be
asked to lay down their 'vehicle.' They didn't
think their bodies were significant."

David Moore grew up in Los Gatos, near
San Jose, but had trouble in a regular public school classroom, and began to lag
behind his classmates. His mother placed
him in an alternative, private high school
that concentrated on practical, hands-on
teaching.

His mother described him as an emotional,
often angry teenager during his youth.

He was barely out of high school when

Bo and Peep were traveling up and down the West Coast, holding recruitment meetings to profess their strange beliefs and win followers.

Moore was inexplicably drawn to The Two, the laid-back messengers of a space-ship fantasy.

"He attended several of their meetings, and felt this was for him," his mother told the newspaper. "He called his brother and said, 'I'm leaving to join this group.'"

He disappeared for seven years.

Though he wasn't skilled when he joined the rag-tag band of UFO cultists, he learned about computers from members of the group, his mother said.

Eventually, Moore had become good enough with computers that he became a certified network engineer for Novell computers.

It was a striking moment of pride for his mother.

"I was so proud of him that he'd done this, he'd studied hard and passed the test," she told the newspaper.

With his new computer skills, Moore got a job in September 1996 at Comp-x

Computer Systems, a computer store in San Diego, where another cult member also worked.

"They were always saying that they lived together, supported and worked for each other," Mike Afshin, the store manager, told the *Washington Post*, praising the pair as both honest and punctual.

"They said they share the money, they share food, that they're religious people, that they do fasting also."

Brown looked and acted anything but brainwashed, his former employer said.

"They were kind of gentle people," Moore's mother said. "I notice this among former members that I've met. They're not what I would consider to be pro-active, assertive-type people. They were taught that people are entitled to what they believe. In fact, I've heard from former members that this was one of the things David had to work on. . . . He had to learn to channel his expression."

But for seven years, Moore's mother was desperate for any word of him. Dark fears made the years unspeakably torturous.

So desperate to find her son—especially

after the 1978 Jonestown massacre—
Brown contacted a cult specialist who
helped her find out that he was alive.

But it would be three more years before she
would see her son. Shortly after, she would
start a support group for other parents of sons
or daughters lost to "Total Overcomers," as the
cult called itself at the time.

There would be just one more visit
between Brown and her long-lost son
before he died.

"The two visits I had with him were very
satisfactory," Brown told the newspaper.
"He was very open. He was obviously very
devoted. It was very clear: This is what he
chose. I did come to a turning point some
years ago—I accepted he was free to choose.
As long as he was not harming himself or
others, I wouldn't interfere."

Brown said her son told her his reclu-
siveness was a necessary part of his new life.
He felt he couldn't be in contact with his
family because it would hurt his group—
"tug at their vibrational level."

Christmas cards came. There were some
phone calls. But over the years, Brown had
really nothing left of her son.

"It's been, I'd say, twenty-one years of losing. It doesn't end. It's layers of an onion. You feel like you come to terms with it, and then something happens, you really find yourself missing them—you wish you could share family news with them—and you have another little experience of loss there. I've been open-ended grieving for twenty-one years."

The tragedy at Rancho Santa Fe cut a terrible swathe across every strata of American family life. The very rich, it turned out, were very much like everyone else—at least when it came to Heaven's Gate.

In the case of David Cabot Van Sinderen, 48, old wealth helped fund the crazy cult's activities.

His ever-present sense of humor cast an even more ghastly pall over the mass suicide.

Eccentric wealthy men are certainly not a rare breed.

Van Sinderen's involvement in the cult may have disturbed the family, but they—like others—had come to accept it.

The world's first glimpse of Van Sinderen came in a startling farewell video played after the cybercult suicides. While other members were grim faced and serious in their messages of farewell, Van Sinderen was gleeful, even silly.

The son of a blue-blood Connecticut family wore a "Cat in the Hat" cap and joked before killing himself that he wondered if he might not be able to reach the controls on the spaceship that would take him to eternal peace.

"It is significant that David wore a 'Cat in the Hat' cap before committing suicide," said his brother-in-law, Richard Abbate of Cheshire, Connecticut.

Abbate said there were no situations in which Van Sinderen could not find the humor, or joke. He was a "gifted artist" who had an endearing, playful sense of humor, Abbate said.

His family's great, old wealth guaranteed there would be no private grieving.

Van Sinderen's seventy-two-year-old father, Alfred, is former chairman of the Southern New England Telephone Company. Though he suffered a cerebral hemorrhage in 1996, family members said he was told of his son's death, and was devastated by it.

With a trust fund set up by his grandfather—who was in the Social Register and who founded the Mayflower Inn in Washington, D.C.—the younger Van Sinderen no doubt helped bankroll the cult's activities.

He had bought the cult a 40-acre former youth camp near Mountainair, New Mexico, on which to live for awhile in 1995. The cult members moved off the ranch, and into the rented three million dollar ranch in Rancho Santa Fe in October 1996.

It was Van Sinderen who co-signed the lease on the death mansion.

The wealth, and all its prestige, meant nothing to him. He had known it all his life.

Van Sinderen was third generation of his family to attend the exclusive Gunnery boarding school in Connecticut, and spent some time in college at Miami before graduating from Oregon State University.

He joined the new recruits of Bo and Peep in 1976 and—like all the cultists—had little more to do with his family or previous life afterward.

The last time they saw David was in 1985, when he visited his sister, Sylvia.

"That time he visited with a fellow friend from the religion and showed us a video," Abbate said. "He seemed happy and was very pleasant."

Last year, there was a phone call.

"He used to call sporadically and let us know he was all right and check on the family," Abbate said. "David was always vague about where he was, usually saying he was traveling, never very specific."

His family never doubted that his horrible, final decision to end his own life with his fellow cult members was made with a clear head, and happily.

"While we did not completely understand or agree with David's beliefs, it was apparent to us that he was happy, healthy and acting under his own volition. It seemed to us that the group members were a supportive family unit and David was spiritually fulfilled in his life with them," the family said in a statement released to the press.

"He loved the out doors and was genuinely concerned about the environment and the future of the planet. He always tried to reassure us not to worry about him—that the lifestyle he had chosen was the right one for him.

"He dealt with us honestly and we respected his wishes. We have missed him and will continue to miss him. . . . To David, wherever you may be, we love you."

Nowhere was the irony of the tragedy more pronounced than in the death of Thomas Nichols, 59, the brother of Nichelle Nichols, the actress who played Lt. Uhura on *Star Trek*.

The classic 1960s television series was revered by the followers of Bo and Peep, a compendium of all the alien and space-age mythology the cult ground up and spewed out as its reason for being.

When it debuted on NBC in September 1966, no one knew what a phenomenon it would create. It ran for just three years, but became one of the few series to prove more popular in reruns. More importantly, *Star Trek* acquired a fiercely loyal following, with fans who almost certainly were responsible for securing the show's renewal for a last year in 1969—and who later wrote more than one million letters to the network protesting its cancellation.

Set in the twenty-third century aboard the starship *Enterprise*, *Star Trek*'s voyagers were commissioned by the United Federation of Planets to embark on a five-year mission to "seek out new life and new civilizations."

There were seventy-eight episodes in all.

The *Enterprise* was staffed by a crew of four hundred, though only eight principals were in the cast: William Shatner as Captain James Kirk; Leonard Nimoy as Science Officer Spock, DeForest Kelley as Dr. Leonard "Bones" McCoy, the medical officer, James Doohan as Montgomery Scott—"Scotty"—the chief engineer, George Takei as Mr. Sulu, the helmsman, Majel Barrett as Nurse Christine Chapel, Walter Keonig as Ensign Pavel Chekov, the navigator, and Nichols as Uhura, the communications officer.

Star Trek was created by Gene Roddenberry, who also served as executive producer. The series spawned eight movies between 1979 and 1996, three other television series: *Star Trek: The Next Generation*, *Deep Space Nine*, and *Star Trek Voyager*, and a Saturday morning cartoon version that ran from 1973 to 1975.

So popular was the series its new fans dubbed themselves "Trekkies," and sponsored annual conventions in the United States and England.

It became profoundly popular with the cybercultists, whose whole philosophy revolved around outerspace travel and other worlds.

It was reported *Star Trek* and *The X-Files*, a popular science-fiction thriller that debuted on Fox in 1994, were the only television the cultists would watch.

So unlike her cool, collected character in the TV series, Nichelle Nichols came unraveled when told of the suicide of her brother.

But after a day in seclusion—at which time she reportedly needed to be sedated to deal with the overwhelming grief—Nichols bravely shared her anguish with the world.

She told CNN her brother "was a highly intelligent and beautifully gentle man" who died "with great dignity."

Nichols, who went from her famous role to the job as pitchwoman for a psychic friends line, said she had lost touch with her brother in the early 1970s, and didn't hear from him until their mother died in 1990.

"He let us know he was well and happy," she said.

The next time he surfaced to family members was in 1994, when Thomas Nichols visited his sister along with fellow cult members.

"He told me their organization was going to go public and asked me what I thought would be the best way to let the world know what they were about and where they were going," she said. "They talked about the great comet that would come some day."

Nichelle Nichols certainly had no reason to be concerned about her brother's fascination with comets and space travel.

Even America's distinguished man of letters, nineteenth-century humorist Mark Twain, was fascinated with comets as a means of interplanetary travel.

"Twain was obsessed with comets," said Justin Kaplan, who wrote the biography of Samuel Langhorne Clemens that won a Pulitzer Prize in 1966.

Two Twain stories—"A Curious Pleasure Excursion," written in 1874, and "Extract from Captain Stormfield's Visit to Heaven," written in 1907, both described extraterrestial voyages aboard comets that could collect "billions" of souls from various worlds.

Twain even presaged Bo and Peep's vocabulary, referring to bodies as "containers" for the soul—the same terminology used by the cult.

Of course, Twain was just kidding about interplanetary travel.

Thomas Nichols was deadly serious.

The *Star Trek* connection was a bizarre one, but somehow put Nichols' death in an understandable perspective.

Not so with John "Mickey" Craig, sixty-three, of Durango, Colorado, whose former business associates were dumbfounded by his sudden rejection of a seemingly stable, happy family life.

Craig, known in the cult as Brother Logan, was a successful land developer and the father of six young children when he joined the cult in 1975, at the height of its recruitment in the West. Yet Craig didn't fit any of the stereotypes of some others who drifted toward the cult in those early days.

He had been a prominent Republican who narrowly lost in a bid for the state

House of Representatives in 1970, and was a successful land developer who owned Wilderness Trails Ranch, a renowned dude ranch north of Bayfield, Colorado.

In an extraordinary—and dramatic— move just before he dropped out of sight, Craig had a Durango lawyer draw up two powers of attorney, one for his wife, Mary Ann, and the other for Larry McDaniel, Craig's former attorney and friend, the *Denver Post* reported.

According to the *New York Times*, the move followed by one week a visit from Dale Mackey, an old college classmate who had been a film editor with MGM studios. Three months earlier, Mackey had attended a recruiting session conducted by Bo and Peep.

McDaniel exercised his power of attorney to transfer all of Craig's property into Mary Anne's name, and when years passed with no word form Craig, his wife finally asked McDaniel to help her obtain a divorce.

"We had to act as though he was going to be gone forever," McDaniel told the *Denver Post*. "Mary Ann had six children to raise, and she had absolutely no idea where

Mickey was or whether he was alive or dead. It was a very difficult situation."

To the residents of the Old West town of 15,000, his departure was shocking.

"He was a totally normal guy until he became a moonie," Roderick Barker, owner of the Strater Hotel, told the *New York Times*. "That's what people used to say—that he was going to the moon."

Banker R.W. Turner, Jr. described him as "a perfect cowboy, always dressed like the Marlboro man, pressed Levis, Stetson hat."

The image, at least in part, won him a role in *Butch Cassidy and the Sundance Kid*, where Craig was the first horseman out of the boxcar in the famous train robbery scene, filmed using the Durango & Silverton Narrow Gauge Railroad. His performance in a minor role in a television series so impressed one director that he was asked to star in his own show.

"He was a tremendously charismatic guy," Gene Roberts, who bought Craig's dude ranch from him in 1970 told the *New York Times*. "A lot of people said he looked like Chuck Connors. Frankly, we thought he was better looking."

He was successful, rich, had six beautiful kids, and a great wife. It doesn't get much better.

Craig didn't totally drop out of sight during his cult years.

He contacted several of his six children on at least three occasions, though he never spoke with his wife again after leaving in August 1975.

Craig's eldest daughter, Cathy Craig Murphy, recalled traveling to Denver to meet with her dad soon after he left the family to join what was then called the Human Individual Metamorphosis. At the time, Murphy said she got her first look at Bo and Peep.

"These were very intelligent, charismatic people," Murphy told the *Denver Post*.

True to their strictures about a complete break from the past, the leaders wouldn't let Craig sit with his daughter during a recruitment presentation at the Denver YWCA, nor would they let him walk Murphy to her car afterward.

"They were very protective of their followers," Murphy told the newspaper. "I don't know if they were afraid of [Craig's] leaving the group or what. But he looked and sounded fine to me. I guess he was just following his beliefs, as strange as they might have seemed."

When Craig disappeared, his family recalled that police were hot on the trail of the group, searching the mountainous contryside for signs of the wanderers camp.

"When you look back, I guess you can see little cracks in the concrete," Craig's banker friend told the *New York Times*, noting that in the early '70s, local real estate was in a downturn and that Craig was "stretched out."

A few months before Craig disappeared, he chartered his banker's airplane to fly to Arizona to see a psychic.

"Obviously he was searching for something," Turner said.

As decades passed, the buzz about the successful land developer who ditched the high life for a flying saucer died down.

Indeed, many locals had forgotten all about Mickey Craig until his face appeared in videos aired on network and cable TV in March 1997.

Not his family.

"For me, he died twenty-two years ago," Mary Ann Craig told the Associated Press. "When we found out he was dead, there was a sense of closure, more than anything for us."

Like so many others, the friends and family of Michael Sandoe, twenty-six, of Abingdon, Virginia, know everything about the beginning and end of his life.

It's what happened to the outgoing, popular young man in between that was so inexplicable—and shocking.

For the first eighteen years of his life in rural southern Virginia, Michael Barr Sandoe had what former teachers and friends recalled as a typical, if sometimes boisterous, childhood and adolescence.

Those who knew him before he graduated from high school in 1989 to join the military said they'd lost contact with him—but never worried he would land somewhere on his feet, and with a smile on his face.

The youth those friends recalled was the cheerful senior class president who was well-liked and on his way to a happy, normal adulthood.

"I don't know what might have happened

to him in the military or something else to change him," high school teacher Michael Lethcoe told the Associated Press.

Lethcoe said Sandoe was a member of a youth service group when he attended high school, and exhibited no signs of trouble that would hint his proclivity for a cult that believed in flying saucers and reincarnation.

"It's such an abnormal occurrence, and he was more of a stable individual," Lethcoe said.

For most of his life, Sandoe lived in Abingdon, a historic town just across the border from Tennessee.

In high school, the tall, slight young man was known as a prankster, always joking with people in a good-natured way. Besides membership in the Key Club, the youth-service group, he also belonged to the French Club in his junior year and was elected class president the next.

To his friends, he was a "regular guy who, like any red-blooded American kid, loved his Ford Mustang and had a steady girl.

"Mike had a lot of friends," one former friend, Shannon Markham, told the AP. "I think Mike was pretty happy with the way things were with himself. He was like any of the rest of us: a little crazy, a fairly daring guy. Sometimes we would run around the neighborhood, pulling practical jokes on people."

Another friend, Jackie Craft, told the AP that even running for class president started off as a joke for Sandoe. But Craft said her friend took it seriously once he won.

"His senior year was really a different year for him," she said. "He gained a lot of respect from people."

He seemed on his way after high school, and enlisted in the Army, where, according to his mother, JoAnne Sandoe, he became a paratrooper and a Ranger.

After the serving in the Persian Gulf war, his mother said her son came back and worked and traveled. But to where, would shock her.

JoAnne Sandoe said she had no idea he joined the Heaven's Gate cult.

For his family and friends, what happened when he left the Army was revealed only after authorities found his official records. For example, Texas driving records showed in the early 1990s Sandoe lived in

Dallas, where some of the other cult members also stayed.

Newspaper articles in 1993 reported a Michael Sandoe was among a group of about thirty-five activists who picketed homes of abortion doctors in Dallas. The paper reported Sandoe and several others were arrested during the protests.

When coroner's officials in San Diego released his name last week, they listed his most recent address as Boulder, Colorado.

His stunned family immediately went into seclusion to try to sort out the happy youth full of promise from the doomed young man who lay dead among other cult loonies.

"I watched the pictures of the bodies on the cots for two days," neighbor Lola Bumgarner told the AP. "Then I heard that Michael was one of them. It's totally different then."

No one seemed more "regular," more the classic girl-next-door, than Denise Thurman, forty-four, who friends recalled as a cute and smart cheerleader who grew up without a care in Locust Valley, a comfortable Long Island suburb of New York City.

Her road to Heaven's Gate was the story of how a sweet young woman with energy and cheer slipped into a middle-aged child, emaciated, and docile.

According to Bill Bleyer, a reporter for *Newsday*, and another friend quoted by the newspaper, Ron Capobianco, the change in the young woman appeared to have started around her senior year at Locust Valley High School.

Before that, Thurman had been friendly and carefree, interested in school activities, although not such an enthusiastic student.

"She was intelligent, she was cute, she was funny," Capobianco said. "I remember her being a clown. She is one of those people who left an indelible memory but then totally dropped out. She was charming."

In her senior year, he said, "She became a very different person than the rest of us."

At that point, Thurman was into eastern philosophies, and tried to interest her friends in the subject. She dropped cheerleading and refused to attend the prom, saying it was "pointless and frivolous," her friend said.

The quotation under her yearbook

picture is from Middle Eastern philosopher Khalil Gibran:

"Love has no other desire but to fulfill itself."

"The last time I saw Denise was in the mid 1970s when I dropped her and her dog off at the entrance to the New Jersey Turnpike after she had graduated from Boston University and decided to hitchhike to the West Coast to see the world," Bleyer wrote.

"We had been solid friends all the way through Locust Valley High School and had become so inseparable that by the time we graduated in 1970 they ran candid shots of me and her back-to-back in the yearbook. We'd hang out at people's houses or at Ransom or Stehli beaches. Sometimes she'd drag me along to concerts by the rock group Ten Years After. She was a big fan of Alvin Lee, their lead guitarist. She was very artistic—I think I still have one of her paintings.

"None of us who knew her at that point had the slightest inkling that she would eventually get involved with cults or anything like it. She was an extremely intelligent, very independent young woman with a finely developed, sarcastic sense of humor.

So the idea of her abandoning her will to some group still seems very foreign. . . .

"She sort of shifted her attention from the cheerleaders and jock group to the music and drugs crowd. After high school, she went off to Boston University, while I went to Hofstra. We'd get together when she'd come home for weekends and during the summer. I went up to Boston to visit her sometimes. After college, she was trying to figure out what to do with her life and she went on a voyage of discovery like Jack Kerouac had done. So I drove her into Manhattan, through the Lincoln Tunnel and dropped her off where Interstate 495 intersects with the New Jersey Tunrpike. I was worried about her, but she was very self-assured.

"Basically, she never came back and never was in touch with me or any of the other people in our group of friends. She did return several years after she hitchhiked away, I think without notice, and visited her family. At that time she was already involved in some cult-like group. In fact, when Jonestown came along, my first reaction was, 'God, I hope she wasn't there.'

"I didn't make the connection this time until I came home from Easter dinner and there were messages from several high school friends. Someone asked me, 'Was I shocked by this?'

"The Denise I knew died twenty-something years ago when she basically severed ties and disappeared. Over the years, I kind of hoped she would come back and show up at my door, but as time went on, that seemed less and less likely. The thought that she's gone for good catches in my throat."

Ironically, about twenty years after Thurman set off on her trip of self-discovery, and found Bo and Peep, another Long Island young woman set off on a similar odyssey, and wound up at the same place as Thurman, living the same life, and dying the same death.

Gail Renee Maeder, twenty-eight, had been a quiet lover of nature and animals while growing up in Sag Harbor, Long Island—a happy-go-lucky, artistic child on the East End of Long Island with her parents and younger brother Dan.

She went to the local elementary school

and graduated from high school in 1987, then enrolled in a design college, Johnson and Wales, in Providence, Rhode Island.

But after a year, she came back because her boyfriend, Chad, was still living in New York. The next year, Maeder seemed to be drifting; she took classes at SUNY Nassau County and SUNY Riverhead but then left and took jobs in various Sag Harbor boutiques.

In 1990, Maeder and her boyfriend told friends and family they were going to check out California.

"She said it was only going to be a short time," said her mother, Alice Maeder.

She saw her family a few more times after that, but was already moving far away from her old life and family. At first, Maeder and her boyfriend worked in a tie-dye factory. Then she opened a small shop featuring handmade crafts called Satori Caravan.

"It was pretty much the hippie-type, bohemian thing," her mother said. "It was funny because we always called her a misplaced hippie."

Maeder kept in touch with her family and returned home in 1991 and 1992 to attend weddings. There was nothing to betray where she was headed, her mother noted.

But in 1993, her drifting landed her at Heaven's Gate.

After breaking up with her boyfriend, she closed her shop and in October 1993, moved to Santa Barbara, her mother said.

"She was living in a trailer, doing some housecleaning," her mother said. "She befriended this guy, Richard, who we later learned was probably the recruiter for the cult."

In September 1994, their daughter sent the family a UFO flier in the mail, and a note:

"I felt like I had outgrown it and I just didn't see the point of it. I wanted to share this with you, although you may not understand. I'm hopeful you will try to see the value I see in my pursuit and maybe even feel proud."

A phone call followed the amazing note, when Maeder was in the Colorado Rockies. She asked if they had received the flier, said she was too busy to come home, and promised to call more often.

More strange letters followed, but the voice behind the words was different—a little of the old Gail and a little of a new young woman spouting cult psychobabble.

"I'm learning through practical daily experience how to fine-tune myself," she wrote in one note.

Her notes offered the family their only glimpse of Maeder's new, strange life:

"It may comfort you to know I'm not participating in any sexual acts. The people I associate with don't drink coffee or alcohol or do drugs."

Another suggested her parents see the movies *Groundhog Day* and *Oh God*. She said she was watching *The X-Files* and *Dr. Quinn: Medicine Woman*.

The last letter came in December 1995:

"I thought you might like to know I'm still kickin'."

She told her family she was busy, "learning to use a computer, singing Christmas carols, and eating chocolate."

Maeder's mother said she went "numb" after learning of her daughter's fate. For a while, she had hoped to learn more about her daughter's life by joining a cult awareness network.

She didn't blame her pleasant, loving child for the decision she made.

She blamed Bo.

"She's a victim here," Alice Maeder said. "She is Applewhite's victim. It's baffling, but when she took that stuff, she really believed she was going to wake up and go on a spaceship."

Chapter

8

LOST SOULS

There was one Heaven's Gate true believer who didn't die in the terrible days of suicide beginning March 24, 1997. Her life ended twelve years earlier.

Bonnie Lu Trusdale Nettles was not only the first cult victim. She was far more importantly the first follower of cult guru Marshall Herff Applewhite.

She was Beep, then Ti, then one of The Two.

But first, Nettles was the Houston, Texas, nurse whose star-gazing obsession set Applewhite on the road to Heaven's Gate.

It was with her encouragement, her

confidence that Applewhite forgot all about rejecting the voices inside of his head, answering them instead to establish his spaced-out New Age cult.

Nettles was constantly by Applewhite's side, preaching with him, recruiting for him, traveling with him.

Her family had little idea of her life—and less still of her death of liver cancer in 1985, some twelve years after Nettles walked out on her old life and into Applewhite's. Nettles's daughter, Terrie, had been living just four hours away.

"I felt like somebody had ripped my guts out," she told the Associated Press, adding that she thought at the time: "Now the answers are gone."

But the answers are all there in the thousands of words the cult wrote on the Internet about their strange beliefs in the "next level" and their quest for a flying saucer ride into space.

It was all, after all, just a compilation of much of Nettle's obsession with the occult and astrology, along with a healthy dose of science-fiction and Christianity. If Terrie Nettles were to read those long sermon-diatribes, she might even recognize her mother's influence as Heaven's Gate's first stargazer.

Nurse Bonnie Nettles had just divorced when she met Applewhite, a music professor. Early one morning in 1973, they went to a nightclub where Terrie, then nineteen, worked.

They announced they were leaving.

"I wasn't allowed to say good-bye. I wasn't allowed to tell her that I loved her and hold her hand," she told the Associated Press. "I felt like Herff prevented that from happening."

That was the last time Terrie and her younger brother, Joe Nettles, saw their mother.

"I remember going down the stairs with her, trying to keep from crying," the forty-four-year-old daughter said. "They just said that God was leading them in a certain direction. They weren't sure exactly where, or what their mission was. But she said it was really big."

Seven months after the farewell, a cryptic letter arrived.

Relying on a fiery Bible passage—Revelation

11:3–13—Nettles tried to explain how she and a sexually tormented, castrated opera singer had become the center of a new universe.

"And I will give power unto my two witnesses, and they shall prophesy a thousand, two hundred and three score days, clothed in sackcloth," the passage begins. "These are the two olive trees and the two candlesticks standing before the God of the earth."

What did it mean?

"That's when they first realized who they thought they were, as the two witnesses," Terrie Nettles told the Associated Press. "I had absolutely no clue as to what she was talking about."

Terrie and Joe Nettles said their mother met Applewhite at the Houston Music Theater Center, where he was a music instructor. They firmly reject reports the two met in a loony bin.

"Their relationship wasn't like a romantic thing, more like a friendship, a platonic thing," the daughter said.

The daughter even found her mother and her partner uplifting, she told *Time* magazine.

"I felt like I was in the presence of an incredible human being. It was like I was being uplifted. I felt privileged to be with my mother and Herff. I was the only one who could talk with them together. Their followers had to talk to them in groups, not individually."

Bonnie Nettles felt her relationship with Herff was fated to be and was predicted.

"A couple of spiritualists said that there was going to be this guy coming into her life," Nettles told *Time* magazine. "And then Herff showed up. They linked up on a spiritual plane."

Nettles probably saw the meeting, the compatibility with Applewhite, as her destiny, having written a novel in junior high about a man who died and went to heaven. Applewhite apparently saw himself as the manuscript's hero, the daughter told *Time*.

After Nettles and Applewhite left Houston in January 1973 to form their cult, communication to Terrie Nettles became infrequent.

Sadder still, in the early 1980s—as her mother's life was coming to an end—the tone of her mother's letters changed, the daughter said.

"I had the feeling that she kind of wanted out. That was my interpretation," she told the news magazine. "It was the way she phrased things."

In 1984, Nettles wrote her daughter again, saying she didn't know how to get out and that "there wasn't a graceful way to leave," *Time* reported.

Then, ominously, the letters stopped.

From then on, Bonnie Nettles's kids would hear on television and in newspapers about their mother's exploits with the weird UFO Cult.

In February 1986, Terrie Nettles, then a student in Houston, tried desperately to reach her mother because Bonnie Nettles's mother had died.

Nettles's followers stonewalled relatives' attempts to contact her.

"We can't give her the message unless you tell us what it is," the younger Nettles recalled being told. "Well, I can't do that because the message that I have is very personal."

The followers hung up on her, the daughter recalled.

A few days later, two followers introducing themselves as Dan and Liv appeared at Terrie's front door, delivering snapshots of her mother, and declaring that Bonnie Lu Trusdale Nettles—Peep—had died nine months earlier.

Robert Balch, went back nine years later to check out the group when it resurfaced.

"The meeting followed the same format I had seen many times in 1975, although here, too, members were more willing to answer questions about their personal lives," Balch wrote in his essay included in the book, *The Gods Have Landed*, edited by James R. Lewis.

"As in 1975, there was no hard-sell, no effort to recruit, only a desire to make people aware of the message. Of the nine members present at the meeting, at least three had joined the group in the last year. I was told that a total of twelve people had joined since the 'final offer' began, but nobody in the audience at this particular meeting was receptive. By the end of the presentation, only myself and two others were left, but the UFO people didn't seem discouraged.

"During the meeting the speakers talked about The Two as if they both were still physically present in their lives, however, Peep had died of cancer in 1985, or as their

followers put it, she had 'left her vehicle'
because her work on the human level was
finished. I had learned about Peep's death
from her daughter, who said Bo had sent
her a tape explaining what had happened.
Despite the group's emphasis on overcoming human attachments, she said Bo
seemed to be crying when he talked about
her. . . . When I asked the members about
this, they didn't see a contradiction. After
all, they explained, even Jesus wept in the
garden of Gethsemane, but that didn't
mean he was attached on the human level.
Yet I still had to wonder about Peep. After
her death, two members delivered her only
possessions to her daughter, including,
ironically, a teddy bear."

Now they are all gone, and it's possible to
see how similar, in some ways, they all
were.

The most recent victims of Heaven's Gate
were smart—like their leaders. Too smart to
be hoodwinked into believing in nonsense
like spaceships and aliens and reincarnation.

Way too smart to die sheepishly, eating
Phenobarbital-packed pudding followed by
a vodka chaser, dressed in black, their heads

in bags, their faces shrouded in flimsy purple cloth.

Bo and Peep's flock was filled with computer whizzes, musicians, teachers, scholars, seekers—sons and daughters, mothers and fathers, sisters and brothers of God-fearing, hard-working Americans.

And lost souls, like Raymond Alan Bowers, forty-five, of Jupiter, Florida.

"He cried all the time," Denny and Karin Nickeson, friends who used to play music with him, told the Associated Press. "He cried all the time."

Bowers was twenty-five when he first heard Applewhite in 1975 in a seminar on UFOs at Stanford University in Palo Alto, California. He followed Applewhite for eight years but broke away, said his sisters, Joy and Susan Ventulette.

But mental anguish from divorce, the death of their younger brother, abuse of drugs and alcohol, drove him back into the cult, the sisters said. Their younger brother had been killed in 1988 on a lobster boat off Connecticut. At the time, Bowers was in a courtroom, getting divorced, and losing custody of his three young kids.

Three years ago, Bowers moved in with his sister Susan in Martin County, did odd jobs, and watched TV. Then he ran into a former cult member, called the meeting "destiny," and returned under Applewhite's wing, his sisters said.

"No one forced him to do this," his other sister Joy told a reporter. "He was with them because he found an inner peace that he could not find in the outside, real world."

Bowers seemed happiest in the outside world when he was playing his guitar and jamming with Denny Nickeson, the friend said.

"He was lost," Karin Nickeson told *USA Today*. "I don't think life meant much for him."

Bowers was arrested once in October 1994 in Florida for possessing cocaine. But that was the least of his troubles.

"He was a spiritual person who saw good in everybody," said his sister Susan Ventulette.

The loneliness—and natural drifting to the structured environment of Heaven's Gate—drew many of the members together.

But there were also examples of followers persuading friends—and in the case of Gary St. Louis—of persuading family to join Heaven's Gate. It was at St. Louis's advice that his half-sister, Dana Abreo joined the cult, their families said.

Gary Jordan St. Louis, forty-four, left his northern Idaho home in 1992 to join the cult, leaving his Coeur d'Alene girlfriend, Shelly King, with his personal belongings and a videotape explaining his decision.

"Today is February 12, 1992. It's Wednesday. I want everybody who may see this, or to know, that I have chosen to leave," he said on the tape. "I want to rejoin my heavenly Father, and my classmates, the students of my heavenly Father. I'm really happy about this. To walk away and begin doing some work for my real Father means more to me than anything."

When he was growing up, he was the last person his friends believed would be joining a cult.

Bright and outgoing, a sudden change came over St. Louis after he graduated in 1971 from Downey High School in Modesto, California.

"He kind of flipped out," family friend
Vicki Zaiger told *USA Today*. "He was brilliant with computers, and he worked for
the government in Colorado for a while.
But he was secretive and didn't keep in
touch with his parents."

When the cult resurfaced from its underground years in the 1980s, St. Louis was a
key player in helping launch Heaven's Gate
into cyberspace.

So convinced was he of the importance of
the cybercult, he even persuaded his half-
sister to follow the spaced-out computer
nerds.

St. Louis's thirty-five-year-old half-sister
grew up in Twain Harte, California, and
moved to Denver after high school to attend
paralegal school.

But from 1990 to 1993, Abreo drifted
from one apartment to another in the east
Capitol Hill area.

"As soon as I heard it, I knew it was
them," Abreo's other half-brother, Gary,
told *USA Today*. "To them, it was the only
way to leave the planet—to leave their bodies behind and escape."

Another lost-soul member, Margaret

June "Peggy" Bull, fifty-three, joined Bo and Pepp from the beginning of their doomed crusade in the mid 1970s. She had graduated from Ellensburg High School, and then the University of Washington with an English degree. She immediately went to Barcelona, Spain, and taught English.

Peggy Bull returned home when her mother died three years ago and told relatives her fellow cultists were self-supporting, drove expensive cars, lived communally, moved frequently and were celibate, her brother said.

"I thought it was harmless," her brother, John Bull, Dean for Continuing Education at Central Washington University in Ellensburg, Washington, told *USA Today*. "But when we received a video from Peggy that had [Applewhite] declaring himself the second coming of Christ and that he intended to lead his flock to redemption, I got a real bad feeling."

Gwen Sorensen, a childhood friend who rode with her in the Wranglerette Riding Club, said it was evident in the early years that Bull was sincerely a "nice person."

"It surprises me she would do this

because she just didn't seem to be the type," Sorensen told the *Ellensburg Daily Record.*

There were other runaways—adults running away from decisions, from life, from past constraints, from future mistakes.

Such was the case of Cheryl Elaine Butcher, forty-three, who fled her hometown of Springfield, Missouri, in 1976 to take up with a group in Oregon led by Applewhite.

The move, her mother Virginia Norton said, made Butcher feel happy.

"She didn't call it a cult. She didn't consider it as a cult. She was happy," Norton told the Associated Press, adding, that she had not seen her daughter since 1993, when she visited her in Dallas.

Norton said her daughter never mentioned suicide, or a belief in UFOs. The mother tried to contact her daughter over the years, but cards and notes came back unopened:

"She was with me for twenty-one years, and with the group for twenty-one years," Norton told *USA Today.*

It was that way for most of the cult members—sons and daughters for about as long as they were slavishly devoted cultists.

Like Erika Ernst, forty.

The native of Calgary, Canada, was described by friends as a good student and fun-loving teenager who joined the cult shortly after graduating from high school.

Then, she gave up all of her belongings and left Calgary for good.

Her family knew she was with the Heaven's Gate cult, but not where. They were vacationing in Los Angeles when they heard of the mass suicide and were the first family to drive to the coroner's office to claim her body.

"For twenty-one years, I tried to find them," her father, Edwald Ernst, said. "We had one visit, maybe one phone call. She told us only that 'I'm doing the best; I'm happy.' But I think she was brainwashed."

Others had tried to live out their dreams, but found their fears leading them straight to the cult.

Darwin Lee Johnson, forty-two, of Utah had played in a rock 'n' roll band called Dharma Combat in Salt Lake City, his former band manager David Fratt said. Fratt said the band was playing in several clubs and that its lyrics spoke of death and aliens.

Some families are left with nothing but their anger and outrage at deaths that made no sense.

"I'm angry she could do this to the family that loved her so much," the foster sister of Julie LaMontagne, forty-five, told the *Boston Herald*.

"She was so brilliant, so intelligent. She had the world," said Kathleen Plourde.

"We feel we lost her twenty-two years ago when she joined that cult. Now we've lost her forever," said her foster mother, Theresa Boucher, who raised LaMontagne from the age of four in Brimfield, Massachusetts.

"The minute I heard about the UFOs on TV, I knew it was the cult she was in. We feel we've lost a daughter."

Nothing about her end made sense to anyone who knew her.

"She was strong, idealistic, intelligent, kind. I remember her as strong and capable," a friend told the *Boston Herald*. "I want people to know that Julie was a great person who was traumatized. There are a lot of people who loved her. She was truly a good human being who was vulnerable."

The friend pointed to a drastic change in LaMontagne's life in 1975, when she saw her best friend die in an accident while on vacation in Mexico.

"She behaved heroically. She tried artificial respiration. She was deeply shaken by the experience. She went out to Oregon to clear her head, and that's when she got picked up by these people. The Two came to town and she took off with them."

It wasn't long after that LaMontagne called her friends in an Amherst house they were all sharing.

"She wanted us to get rid of her earthly possessions," the friend told the newspaper. "We told her we didn't want to. We wanted her to come back. We were very concerned. She told us all about the cult. We knew about the Higher Level, we knew about the UFOs. She told us about Bo and Peep. When she would call, she'd have quite a bit of urgency in her voice. The spaceship was coming soon."

LaMontagne had two biological brothers and two foster siblings who were all raised with Louis and Theresa Boucher, along with the Boucher's biological son.

"There isn't a day that has gone by we haven't prayed she would come out of that cult," Theresa Boucher said. "They weren't prisoners as such, but they were prisoners of the mind.

"I don't know how they hooked her. She always wanted to help and heal people. They must have pushed the right button to make her feel she could make a difference in the world."

The cult member's natural mother, who was ill, was devastated by the news of her daughter's suicide.

Now, the extended family wonders what happened for the ten years their loved one who renamed herself "Faith" simply dropped out of sight.

"She talked about UFOs. She believed in a higher level. We just thought she was brain-washed," Plourde told the *Boston Herald*. "We talked to her. We tried to get her out of there. But she was happy. This was her life and we had to respect that. It didn't seem as though it was dangerous. We didn't' know any of this would happen. We're just as shocked as the world is."

There was another thing that linked

LaMontagne to the other lost souls of Heaven's Gate.

"She was always searching for something," Plourde said. "She was brilliant. She had different ideas. She always wanted something more out of life. I was a domestic person, content to stay home. She thought she could cure the ills of the world."

LaMontagne's brother, Andrew, of Windsor, Vermont, said his sister had plans to be a nurse when she graduated in 1974 from the University of Massachusetts–Amherst nursing school. But then her father died, plunging her into despair.

"She thought he was her knight in shining armor," her brother told the Associated Press. "When he passed away, Julie just freaked out. And then she met those people, and it was all over."

He said his sister acted as a personal nurse to Applewhite.

"This was just the final loss." he said of Applewhite. "Look at the guy, he looks like a lunatic. He's a monster. He took my sister."

Jackie Leonard, seventy-two, was the oldest among the victims. She grew up in

Des Moines, Iowa, and raised two daughters and a son there with her late husband.

Her son-in-law, Angelo Bellizzi of Seattle, said she was "always groping and looking for something that interested her."

In the early 1970s, she moved to Colorado, where she met members of Applewhite's cult and, a few years later, joined the group in San Francisco.

"Grandmothers don't run away," Bellizzi told *USA Today*. "The kids are supposed to run away."

Yet Leonard always seemed to be restless—another lost soul searching for a home.

In the exact same abrupt way—leaving friends and relatives to wonder what had gone wrong, Jeffrey Howard Lewis, forty-one, sold his possessions and left San Antonio to join Heaven's Gate in 1993.

Beforehand, he had been a massage therapist who had worked out of his house.

His friend, David Tayloe, said when Lewis chose the cult, he rejected everything and everyone from his old life.

"He told us that he wouldn't be communicating with any of his friends and to be happy for him, because this is what he felt was right for him," Tayloe told the AP.

Tayloe said it was the second time Lewis had joined the cult.

Lewis's brother, Jerry, said his brother joined first in the mid 1970s after Navy duty in San Diego, and was a member for ten years. He then left, and rejoined.

"Even when he was out of the cult, he talked about it a lot," his brother told *USA Today*. "He had a lot of emotional ties, and he felt he didn't have the meaning that he had when he was in the group."

Families' reactions to their loved one's recruitment by the cult varied, but for the family of Joel Peter McCormick, it was instant panic.

The twenty-nine-year-old had graduated from Malcolm Shabazz City High School in Madison, Wisconsin, in 1986, and joined a group then called the Total Overcomers in Seattle on May 16, 1994.

His roommates called to tell his mother they hadn't seen him for ten days, and Megan McCormick drove nonstop from Madison to Seattle to find her son.

She said she was "reasonably certain that

Joel is physically all right," but said she somehow knew he would be "irrevocably changed if and when he comes out."

When she arrived in Seattle, the mother found her son had joined the UFO cult. He later wrote his mother saying:

"I'm doing fine and continue to grow toward the future."

When his black-shirt, black-pant and black sneaker-clad body was found, McCormick was carrying a driver license with a Salt Lake City address, authorities said.

The stars. The stars. The stars drew everyone together in life, and in death.

So it was for Norma Jeane Nelson, fifty-nine. But her star-gazing was considered way overboard by her shocked North Dallas neighbors who listened to her tales about being from the TV show *Star Trek*.

"We just looked at her in surprise. It just didn't dawn on us that she was in a type of cult," neighbor Cynthia McGowan told *USA Today*. "We thought that maybe she was crazy."

That was by far the exception. Many of a core group of the faithful were merely crazy about computers.

Margaret Ella Field Richter, forty-six, was valedictorian at Las Plumas High School in Oroville, California, in 1969. She was also a Presidential Scholar and a National Merit Scholarship winner.

Her sister, Jean Long, said Richter was a bona fide whiz kid, majoring in computer science, math and German at the University of California at Berkeley, and graduating in just three years.

A quick marriage—it lasted just three years—ended and Richter went to Los Angeles in 1975 to earn her master's degree in computer science at UCLA.

Then, Richter seemed to disappear from view, maintaining little contact with her relatives.

Over the next twenty-two years, Richter visited relatives in Oroville just twice.

Richter "would write letters and she was concerned for us," Long told *USA Today*. "It never sounded like they were going to hurt themselves. . . . It never sounded violent in any way."

Long had idolized her sister, and found the long silences unbearable.

"She was so smart," Long recalled.

Her high school counselor, Jane Hammer, told *USA Today:*

"She just had this extreme mental power. She was involved in all these things. She was very friendly, very open and very outgoing."

Susan Frances Strom, forty-four, was another smart energetic youth when she turned her back on a privileged comfortable family to join the UFO freaks.

Born the daughter of retired U.S. District Judge Lyle Strom of Omaha, Nebraska, Strom loved plants, animals and the Earth, and had planned a career in botany.

Her dad thought her fascination with the cult, which she joined in 1975, was merely a phase.

"I thought, sure it would be short-lived and she would be back home," he told *USA Today.*

He said he is as mystified by why the athletic, intelligent woman—the second oldest in a family of seven—was drawn to the cult as others were stumped at how their loved ones could follow such insanity.

"I have no answers," Strom said. "It did not seem consistent with her character and personality."

Strom graduated from an all-girls school,

Marian High School in Omaha, in 1971, and was attending Oregon State University in Corvallis, Oregon, when she joined the cult in her senior year.

In at least one case, the cult members became fixtures in a small town in New Mexico.

One, Susan Elizabeth Nora Paup, fifty-four, befriended a little girl who still misses "Nora."

In September 1995, Paup was one of the signers on the lease for a piece of property cult members used as a compound in Manzano, New Mexico, for $3,400 a month—the same mountain retreat the group abruptly left in April 1996, just before they settled in San Diego County.

In nearby Mountainair, six group members also rented, for $250 a month, three offices for computer work.

Nora left Rachel a gift when she left—a wooden statuette of an elephant, black with white tusks. Nora knew that Rachel liked elephants because the girl had drawn some while hanging around Nora's office.

Along with the elephant was a note in which Nora told Rachel good-bye and that she hoped to be back the next spring.

Nora never came back. The next time Rachel saw her friend, her face was on the television along with thirty-eight other people who had committed mass suicide.

The little girl ran into the bathroom of her grandmother's house and used up a whole roll of tissue paper to dry her tears.

It was a short friendship, but a deep one.

Here's how it grew.

Nora and five other members of the Heaven's Gate cult ran their computer business in three offices adjacent to Gustin Hardware on Mountainair's main drag.

It was an unlikely spot for a high-tech business: three small spaces attached to an old-fashioned hardware store with wood floors and deer trophies mounted on the wall behind the counter.

"The phone company had to come in and do a lot of work to get the offices ready," Darrell Roberts told the *Albuquerque Tribune*.

One day, the group members arrived with a U-Haul full of computer equipment. No one was quite sure what they were up to since they only said they contracted with other companies to do computer work.

But little Rachel, who tags after her

mother, Patti Heard, as she cleans the hardware store, wasn't afraid, and had an energetic interest in computers. She noticed the new guys right away.

"I said, 'You must be new,'" Rachel told the *Tribune*. She said, 'Yeah, I'm Nora.' I told her my name. I asked her, 'Do you work on computers a lot?' She said, 'Yeah.' I sat by her and I watched her as she worked on stuff. She used a mouse and clicked on different names."

Nora started giving Rachel scrap paper to draw on while her mother cleaned. Rachel presented her new friend with her crayon renditions of animals and mountains. "I guess she took them with her," Rachel said.

Once, Nora gave Rachel a red box for storing her art work.

But mostly, the older woman and the little girl talked about everyday things—and flying saucers too.

"She said she liked UFOs," Rachel said. "I thought, 'OK, she likes UFOs.' In this town, it's not that strange. She'd say they're pretty neat and that she'd seen some. She said maybe sometime we could go out in the field and see one."

The busy cult workers followed a strict routine while they worked. They arrived at eight every morning in a white van, and worked quietly at their computers, ate lunch together from a cooler of fruits and vegetables and left at five on the dot.

"They didn't stand out there and chat," said Denise Roberts, motioning toward the atrium between the offices. "They all had their jobs."

When they first arrived in Mountainair, the men had shaved heads and the women wore their hair very short. They all wore black pants and white smocks. But they soon started varying their wardrobes.

"They told me someone had mentioned they looked kind of cultish," Darrell Roberts told the newspaper.

They offered to help with the Roberts's computers and were happy to exchange pleasantries but only occasionally offered anything about themselves. "They talked about raising money for a monastery up there where they lived," in a compound near Manzano some twelve miles to the north, Darrell Roberts said.

Another time, Nora once confided in Denise Roberts.

"She said the pressure she had felt before she got with this group was not pleasant," Roberts said. "She was happy with what she was doing. That was as personal as it ever got."

But it was different between Nora and Rachel.

Nora talked to Rachel about schoolwork and showed her how to play solitaire on the computer.

"I felt remorseful that I didn't say more that could have helped how ever they were feeling," Denise Roberts told the *Albuquerque Tribune*. "I liked them."

Darrell Roberts cried when he realized the connection. "It was hurtful," he told the newspaper. "Such a waste of nice people's lives."

All told, the Heaven's Gate members stayed for six to eight months before they pulled up stakes for California.

"When they got ready to go, it was almost overnight," Denise Roberts told the newspaper. "They said they were 'called' or 'summoned' to California."

For the most part, cult members rejected any social contact with non-group members.

If they talked at all, it was sometimes just half-truths.

Nancy Dianne Nelson, forty-five, of Mesa, Arizona, told everyone she was a nun who lived in a monastery with two men who were highly knowledgeable about computers.

Her driver's license said Nelson lived in a mobile home in Scottsdale, Arizona, but in the osteopathic surgeon's office where Nelson worked during periods in 1995 and 1996, friends knew little about her—and nothing about her cult.

There was still a frustrating lack of detail about the lives of the other cult victims.

They were identified as: Gordon Thomas Welch, 50, of Arizona; Lawrence Jackson Gale, 47, Lake Forest, California; Alphonzo Ricardo Foster, 44, Detroit; Lindley Ayerhart Pease, 41, of New Hampshire; Suzanne Sylvia Cooke, 54, of New Mexico; Steven Terry McCarter, 41, Albuquerque; Lucy Eva Pesho, 63, Brian Alan Schaaf, 40, Joyce Angela Skalla, 58, all of New Mexico; Robert John Arancio, 46, Michael Howard Carrier, 48, and Betty Eldrie Deal, 64, all of Texas.

The deaths of the cultists in California shocked the nation, but no more than they did Aaron St. Pierre, a cult dropout.

"I thought they left in the fall of 1976, I was sure of it," St. Pierre said. "All these years I thought I had missed the boat, that they had left without me. Then, I was floored when I saw Applewhite on TV, I was floored."

His life's pattern is the one the others might have followed had they not held onto their slim hopes of hitching a ride on a comet.

St. Pierre, now a forty-one-year-old registered nurse in Oregon, was just a teen when he was recruited to join Heaven's Gate in 1975. He traveled across the U.S. with them, praying, recruiting other followers—and waiting for the flying saucer to take him to God.

All the while, St. Pierre said he truly believed Applewhite's repeated claims that he was the son of God and that he and his chosen few would be flown to Heaven imminently.

In September 1976, Bo announced the reason a UFO hadn't already come for his

eighty-odd followers were that some of
them weren't praying hard enough.

"The whole group was to search their
souls and see if they were holding the rest
back by not trying hard enough," he
recalled.

St. Pierre, who had taken a vow of
chastity to join the group, admitted that
the lusty feelings he had for a couple of the
female recruits was interfering with his
prayer time.

Unlike recent followers who had themselves castrated, St. Pierre said the idea of
genital mutilation never came up then.

"If someone had told me to do it at the
time, I probably would have, that's the state
of mind I was in," he admitted. "I realized I
was unworthy and I had to leave. About a
dozen of us left."

As he was leaving, St. Pierre said he was
told the rest of the group would be "picked
up" within a matter of weeks.

"It was crushing for me to leave, I felt I
had given up my only opportunity for an
eternal life," he said.

He's married now, and he no longer has
such strong doubts about his choices. But

Bo and Peep still seem to have an iron hold on him.

"I didn't understand why they committed suicide. They promised we would not die, that we would leave in our physical bodies, that we would remain alive," he said.

But even after learning about the suicides, St. Pierre thought there might be a chance, just the slightest chance, of the resurrection Bo also promised.

"He promised he would come back. He didn't. I don't know what to believe," he said.

There seems no way to turn your gaze toward earth once you've stared into the stars.

Chapter

9

THE AFTERMATH: WHAT'S GOING ON HERE?

Experts have argued about cults for years—what makes them tick, why people are drawn to them and how they effect society. The monstrous deed of Marshall Applewhite and his UFO-obsessed computer geeks adds more fuel to the always fiery controversy.

Like other mindless acts by disturbed cult groups, the strange legacy of Heaven's Gate is bound to leave a blemish on the American Dream.

Why would thirty-nine people suddenly feel such a void as to make a final, frightening exit? Most of these thirty-nine lost souls grew up just like the rest of us—being educated in good schools, working the same jobs and having the same childhood dreams.

What happened? Has the American Dream turned into an irreversible nightmare? The interpretations are endless.

Asking many of the questions—as they were pummeled with inquiries by their parishioners—were ministers around the country. The issue in religious circles was particularly a hot one coming around Easter.

Some pastors dismissed mentioning the mass suicide as irrelevant or inappropriate for a service on the Resurrection.

"This is just news," said Pastor Mark Taylor of Christian Renewal Church in Stockbridge, Georgia. "There's no association between the cult and mainstream Christianity."

Obadiah Harris, president of Philosophical Research Society in Los Angeles, which practices non-sectarian universal spirituality, mentioned the tragedy in a lecture because of calls he's received.

"I think they have found themselves

fascinated with death to the riddle of life. Life goes on and it is not solved by death, it is solved by learning and going on. I don't think you can take the gates of heaven by storm, not even in a space-ship," he said.

Sadly, most authorities agree. The mind-boggling acts committed in the lush hillside mansion in Rancho Santa Fe will not be the last such shocking act of its kind.

There will always be charismatic leaders like Marshall Applewhite, Jim Jones and David Koresh to prey upon the weak, the dissatisfied, the confused person looking for answers.

"Jim Jones's last words to his followers was 'We will meet in another place' and his followers drank the poisoned Kool-Aid because they thought they were going to heaven," cult expert Jim Siegelman told Reuter.

Siegelman, co-author of *Snapping: America's Epidemic of Sudden Personality Change,* said a cult's main job is to tear down its members already fragile personalities and egos. Then, the subject is trapped.

"These can be bright well-educated

people who are in a major life transition," he wrote.

"They have left home for the first time, they have just broken up with a lover, they are feeling lonely and suddenly they are greeted by a smiling, supportive stranger who offers them feelings of love and bonding and who radiates happiness and spiritual fulfillment."

New recruits are isolated, deprived of rest, and beaten down with mind control techniques which makes them susceptible and vulnerable to virtually any command.

And they are willing to believe *anything* that is told to them—strange tales of rebirth, afterlifes in outerspace, transferals into new bodies.

"The people who commit mass suicide under mind control do not think they are going to die. They think they are going to meet angels or aliens or be lifted up to heaven," Siegelman told Reuter.

Siegelman said the introduction of computers and the World Wide Web into the seduction and recruitment of cult members—a technique the Heaven's Gate cultists made use of—is a frightening new development.

"There are not just sexual predators on the net, but spiritual ones as well," he said.

To Ronald Enrich, an expert on new religious movements, an emotional timebomb went off inside Applewhite, and his flock followed him like sheep into oblivion.

"To put it in very unprofessional, unacademic language, it looks as if somebody snapped—probably the leader. Some emotional trigger occurred and these people followed suit," Enrich said.

It is not at all surprising that most of the cultists were young, said the sociology professor.

"That age bracket is precisely the target population for cults. Eighteen to twenty-six is the group that most of the new organizations are targeting," Enrich said.

"And if it is in an upscale neighborhood, the new groups have been targeting the upper middle class."

There is another troublesome aspect to the Heaven's Gate tragedy—the gay issue.

Applewhite, who was either bisexual or gay, apparently was struggling to quash his feelings. If, in fact, self-hatred over his apparent homosexuality was what led Applewhite to castrate himself, form Heaven's Gate, then command other men to have the same surgery, should his orientation be blamed for the end result?

A resounding "no", gay activists insisted.

Gays said there were numerous other issues that could have led to the tragedy.

"When I first heard this story I said to myself, 'I wonder where the gay angle is going to come in,'" said Allen White, a San Francisco publicist and gay activist who came out in the 1970s.

"But in this case the guy was simply nuts, and what's really crazy about this is you wonder why so many people would follow such a nut."

A large number of gays deal with a hostile society and mixed emotions much more maturely than Applewhite did, said Roy Aarons, founder of the National Lesbian and Gay Journalists Association.

"I was a totally scared, closeted gay person back in the '70s. But I was not talking about beaming up to a spaceship somewhere, fortunately," he recalled.

Reports indicate that Applewhite began leading a double life away from his wife and two children in the late 1960s, during which he jumped into a number of gay affairs with younger men.

When he later became obsessed with outer space, he adopted vows of celibacy which led to a self-castration.

Aarons said while Applewhite's sexual identity crisis may have pushed him to some of his beliefs the suicides couldn't really be hung on his homosexual experiences.

Aarons said the 1970s were tough for gay society. It wasn't until 1973 that the American Psychiatric Association switched its position that being gay was a mental illness.

Janja Lalich, a specialist in psychological influence and cults, told the *San Francisco Examiner:*

"Most cult leaders will take their hangups and make them the focal point of the group. Clearly, it was a tormented identity that he had."

Lalich said Applewhite's castration was driven by self-hate because, "if you're hating yourself and these feelings you're having, and there's no outlet that you can be accepted in society, you cut it off. You cut it off symbolically by putting it in the back of your head—and you also do it physically."

But are misguided leaders completely to blame for leading others to the slaughter?

"These people do have free wills," said Gerald McDermott, a college professor of religion and philosophy.

"They are influenced by the leaders, yes. That doesn't mean their minds have snapped or they have been coerced. It means they have found something or someone who accepts their search for transcendence."

Jim Jones, the son of the crazed Peoples Temple leader who led 913 followers to die by swallowing cyanide-laced Kool Aid, said the power of a leader boils down to his dynamics.

"I think the charisma is the icing on the cake. We have great manipulators all around us," Jones told CNN.

"They're opportunists, and they see that some people need to have a vision or a dream. And they take the opportunity to manipulate them."

But it does appear, at least to detectives, that every member of Applewhite's brood approved 100 percent of their ultimate act together.

"This is not like Waco or Jonestown. Each one did this of their own volition even though they were in a cult," said Dick Joslyn, who left the Heaven's Gate sect after fifteen years.

R. Scott Appleby, an expert on new religious movements at Notre Dame University, agreed.

"These charismatic leaders have reached these people at a very different level. There's been some kind of very radical transformation of their heart. These people weren't converted because they said, 'This is the kind of idea I've been looking for—a comet that hides a spaceship,'" Appleby said.

Applewhite once made a crack about people who strived to find somebody else to believe in. In a feature article in the 1970s, he wrote: "Some people are like lemmings, who rush in a pack into the sea and drown themselves. They join any movement. Some people will try anything."

Joe Szimhart, a cult "exit counselor"

based in Pottstown, Pennsylvania, told the
Washington Post:

"If the leader sounds confident, there's a
certain percentage of people who are going
to be infected by that confidence. They're
going to trust and take the next step, which
is to suppress doubt."

New York University Medical Center psychiatrist Marc Galanter said people who join
a cult can suffer from disillusionment, but
they will fight to suppress it.

"They're in a vice. If they try and move
out, they may feel worse. But if they get
more involved, they feel good. So they tend
to get more and more drawn in," Galanter
said.

"New identities are grafted onto old
ones," said Louis Jolyon West, professor of
psychiatry at the UCLA School of Medicine.
"These people take on the identity of smiling happiness about the cult and its way of
life, a kind of superficial quality, almost like
an indifference to the reality that their
career is gone, their parents are in anguish.
A blandness."

Cult expert Larry Trachte, chaplain of
Wartburg College in Waverly, Iowa, noted

the solemn behavior of the cultists and their serious attitudes toward life and recreation, particularly sex.

"These are not the kind of people who are going to sit down in a coffee shop and have an intimate conversation with a member of the opposite sex," Trachte said.

"They were creating another kind of reality in their mind. It's one thing to relate to a computer screen. It's another thing to engage with another person.

"When you listen to them and watch them on tape, most of them seem to have problems relating to people. At the center of all these groups is a strong need to belong. A need for order.

"These people [seemed] so naive and so gullible. They really [had] difficulties talking about who they are, and relating to their sexuality."

Paul Ginnetty, an associate professor of psychology at St. Joseph's College in Patchogue, New York, hinted the cultists pulled a gigantic cop-out.

"Clearly it's more comforting and exciting to be swept away than to stick around and help with the unglamorous business of rebuilding our inner cities, our waning sense of civility, or even their own fractured familial relationships," Ginnetty said in a column for *Newsday*.

"More authentic religious inspirations would challenge this schizoid and solipsistic stance. One suspects that Mother Teresa, sick as she has been, will not be sending for Dr. Jack Kevorkian—a truly compassionate spiritual outlook suggests that there's still a lot of work to be done.

"Ultimately, the more authentic, life-affirming religious manifestations hang in there amid, and despite, the darkness of human striving."

Suicide-preaching cult leaders and their impressionable flock aside, there is also the theory that physical environment plays a role in helping cults and their unusual ideologies cultivate.

California has the biggest reputation for being a user-friendly place for kooks. But so does the western United States. More cults and fringe groups spring up there than anywhere else in the country.

New Mexico for example.

"A lot of people have the feeling there is

something special or spooky about New Mexico," said Jack Kutz, author of *Mysteries & Miracles of New Mexico*.

"There's an acceptance here," he said. "Instead of being laughed at you are more apt to find a kinship. You might not be considered an oddball but someone who actually fits in."

Some residents believe that federal officials covered up the crash of a large flying saucer near Roswell in 1947.

In northern New Mexico, thousands of believers trek up windy mountain roads to scoop up what is said to be dirt with the ability to heal diseases at the Santuario de Chimayo church.

One woman who lives in Madrid, New Mexico, and answers only to the name of Flow insisted people are drawn to the state by horse spirits.

"There are a lot of horses here. They call to us. And we are a power point. Probably the whole state of New Mexico is a vortex," Flow said.

Some say Applewhite's group may very well have been a second-rate spinoff of a 1970s cult that disbanded after its planned meeting with aliens from outer space never happened.

"One theory that seems to be emerging is that it is a spin-off, derivation or a copycat cult of one of the first UFO cults, which was originally called the Bo Peep Cult," author Siegelman wrote.

"The Bo Peep cult was a mobile cult that floated in the Pacific Northwest and West Coast, especially where it believed it was going to rendezvous with extraterrestrials and aliens who were waiting to meet with them."

Cult experts said some names on the Heaven's Gate website sounded like derivations of Bo and Peep.

"They had names, like Do and Ti and their affiliation with UFOs indicates there might be some connection or members from the earlier group," wrote Siegelman who has spoken with members of the Bo Peep cult over the years.

"We've spoken with people in that group and many were troubled for years afterwards and were not sure of what reality they were in."

Sadly, cult experts warn, more such tragedies lay ahead in the next few years.

"As the millennium approaches, we're getting thousands of these totalitarian groups with apocalyptic visions of reality," said Boston-based cult expert Chip Berlet.

Yet as bizarre cults increase in number, watchdog groups are losing their teeth—pulling back from their open criticism of cults for fear of multi-million dollar lawsuits.

"Unfortunately, there's now very few resources to study and track them," said Berlet, a senior analyst with Political Research Associates and an expert in "apocalyptic hysteria."

The groups are hesitant to lobby against specific cults, for fear of being sued, said Berlet and other cult scholars. The Cult Awareness Network in Chicago was, until recently, the nation's premiere cult watchdog. It was driven out of business by litigation brought by Scientologists.

Unfortunately, the services of watchdog groups are needed now more than ever, according to Berlet.

"As we approach the year 2000, with its rotund significance, all kinds of religious movements are looking at it as a time of possible violence, or cataclysm, or mass suicide," he said.

"We're in for some very unusual behavior in the coming years," agreed Richard Landes, director of the Center for Millennial Studies in Boston.

"It won't stop in the year 2000," Landes said. "We'll be dealing with it for probably decades."

Compounding everything is the ease of communication over the Internet, which Landes called, "The petri dish of prophetic and apocalyptic discourse."

Talk of the apocalyptic significance of a "spaceship" connected to the comet began online as early as last summer, Landes said.

"We don't know what they were expecting. But my guess is that at least at first, they were expecting something else."

No one knows exactly how many cults exist in America, although unscientific estimates put the range from two-thousand to five-thousand. Of the several hundred regularly tracked by experts, a sizable percentage—perhaps as high as half—have apocalyptic beliefs in which the end of the world is forecast.

The approach of the year 2000 will add fuel to those teachings, particularly those of Bible-based, Christian-offshoot groups, experts said.

New Age cults and right-wing, anti-government militias may also be finding significance in the coming turn of the century, they said.

"This is only to be expected. There will be more of this as the end of the century nears," said Stjepan Mestrovic, a sociology professor at Texas A&M University and author of a book on the coming millennium.

The last millennium change one-thousand years ago brought with it mass suicides and religious purges, he said. As the twentieth century neared, there were numerous suicides all over the world by highly educated people.

"The millennium has always had a mysterious, cosmic edge to it, and everyone feels it," Lalich said.

And the Internet is helping fuel millennium fever. Lalich said cult proselytizers troll the Internet, read e-mail and other messages to find likely prospects for conversion.

But the Internet can be used against cults as well, Lalich said, as anti-cult activists create websites to fight cult propaganda, warn new converts, and publicize cult evil.

But is there really any way to keep America's young people from falling prey to the madness? Is there any surefire plan to cult-proof kids?

Maybe not, but parents can provide some of the strongest immunity for their impressionable brood right at home, experts say.

"The best antidote is maintaining relationships with family and friends," said James Fox, dean of Northeastern University's College of Criminal Justice.

Cults cast their nets for "people who are alienated, lonely, isolated, unhappy, or bored, and if your child fits that description, you have work on your hands even if a cult's not nearby."

Clever cultists prey on the vulnerable and "offer them unconditional acceptance and a feeling of belonging they don't get elsewhere," Fox said.

An alert parent is often the first to sense when a son or daughter has slipped into the clutches of a controlling group, said William

Goldberg, a New Jersey–based clinical social worker who works with former cult members and their families.

"One parent told me, 'It's like *The Invasion of the Body Snatchers*. My son looks the same. He says the same things, but something is missing,'" he said.

Some red flags are a suddenly secretive teen who hangs around with a new crowd and drastically changes his or her personality, habits, and hobbies.

There are many organizations parents can turn to for help, including the Cult Information Service, of which Goldberg is president.

"Any of us under the proper set of circumstances could get involved with a cult," he said, noting that "anyone who is in a transitional stage may be vulnerable."

Increasingly, sophisticated recruiters—who prowl the Internet as well as college campuses—sometimes have the most luck with brainy people, said Rabbi Gary Bretton-Granatoor.

"The people one would think are least likely—smart and creative—are often the most successfully targeted," said the rabbi, former director of the Union of American Hebrew Congregations' committee on cults and missionaries, and author of *A Jewish Response to Cults*.

He urged parents to teach children what to look out for about such groups and also encourage them to "have a better sense of self, which is the best defense against a cult."

While much of interpretation of what happened in Rancho Santa Fe was intelligent and carefully thought out, there was some visceral and tasteless reaction from blowhards who love to spout off about everything.

One well known figure who runs one of the world's biggest media companies had jaws dropping when he entered the fray.

"A good way to get rid of a few nuts" media mogul Ted Turner declared.

"There are too many nuts running around anyway, right?" the vice chairman of Time Warner Incorporated blurted out. "It's a good way to get rid of a few nuts. You know, you gotta look at it that way."

Experts who counsel families of cult members immediately blasted Turner for

making "irresponsible, disrespectful statements."

"I'm actually quite surprised that someone of Turner's stature would shoot off his
mouth that way," said Dr. Jim Richardson, a
professor of sociology and judicial studies
who has written extensively on new religions.

"Most of these families are devastated."

Turner said nothing about the shell-
shocked families in his lengthy rant.

"Well, they did it peacefully," he acknowledged. "At least they didn't do like these
S.O.B.s that go to McDonald's or post offices
and shoot a lot of innocent people and then
shoot themselves. At least they went out and
just did it to themselves.

"You know, twenty-nine people, thirty-
nine people committed suicide to go up to
the comet. Well, what about the other six
billion that didn't, you know? That's a small
percentage, thirty-nine out of six billion."

Turner apologized for his remarks a few
days later, but not before they outraged several religious groups, coming just a day
before Easter Sunday.

A spokesman for John Cardinal O'Connor,

leader of the Archdiocese of New York, said the comments by the millionaire known as the "Mouth of the South" were a low blow.

"I can't believe he really meant it, putting such a low value on human life," spokesman Joseph Zwilling said.

The remarks by Turner, the founder of CNN and number two man at Time Warner, fell squarely into his long tradition of making bizarre and sometimes offensive statements on sensitive issues.

He once compared News Corporation Chairman Rupert Murdoch—one of his chief competitors in the cable TV business field—to Adolph Hitler.

During a speech to foreign journalists earlier last year, Turner said the United States "has got some of the dumbest people in the world."

President Clinton took a completely different view.

In his weekly radio address, President Clinton blamed a sense of isolation for triggering the suicides. He said the Easter season was a time to remember that "there are some Americans who feel isolated from all of the rest of us sometimes with truly tragic

consequences like the events just outside San
Diego which has so stunned us all this week."

So much for subtle and sober reflection.
Over on the Internet, a group of computer
fans out of San Diego, disgusted with media
coverage, posted a spoof of the cult's World
Wide Web site, ridiculing Heaven's Gate
members and journalists.

Fake ads hawked "Jelly-O Vodka Pudding
Pops" as "your one-way ticket to paradise."

Hollywood legend Tony Curtis threw his
two cents in, insisting the real reason the
Heaven's Gate clan started committing suicide on March 24, Oscar night, was because
they were diehard members of the Lauren
Bacall Fan Club.

In a mission statement, an unidentified
web designer wrote: "We felt the press put a
ridiculous spin on this thing when they
began alleging that being a webmaster or
webgroup had a dang thing to do with it.

"If they were garbagemen, would the
story be focused on dumps and not the
deaths?"

"There's nothing on TV but this story,"
said Mike Emke, president of a San Diego-
area Internet developer that hosts the site.

"It irritated me."

Art Bell of Pahrump, Nevada, got a weird feeling when he learned of the tragedy, because the talk show host had aired, then discounted, a theory of a UFO trailing the Hale-Bopp comet.

In November, an amateur astronomer told Bell he had a photo showing a mysterious "Saturnlike object" trailing the comet. While astronomers later dismissed it as a star, the rumors continued for weeks.

They were fostered by continued publicity on the Internet and Bell's "Coast to Coast" program, which dealt with reports of a "companion star" operated by aliens that were hiding behind Hale-Bopp.

Bell, who broadcasts from his home, said he was stunned and saddened by the deaths, but added they weren't his problem.

"The Internet is rife with rumors of all kinds of crap. It might not have come from me. Why do people commit suicide? How do you explain the inexplicable?" he asked.

The Heaven's Gate tragedy also sparked a mini-emergency for one of the nation's most visible manufacturers—the Nike sneaker company.

Nike company officials were on pins and needles as the tragedy unfolded even though they didn't want to admit it. Their famed footwear was suddenly taking a beating the way Kool Aid, Tylenol, and McDonald's had in recent tragedies involving their own brands.

A flood of tasteless jokes and comments surfaced about the vivid TV images of brand-new Nike sneakers on the feet of the mass suicide victims in California. The sneakers—with the brand name conspicuously visible—were shown in closeup on the police videotape that was broadcast across the nation.

Soon, computer fans, comedians, and even Wall Streeters—notorious for their ability to come up with mindbogglingly appalling jokes for every occasion—were making fun of Nike's weird notoriety.

One e-mail message posted on the Internet cited Nike's ubiquitous slogan "Just Do It" and said the cult's leader known as "Do"—pronounced Doe—was actually doing an endorsement, saying "Just Do(e) It."

Another e-mailer, noting that Nike is the goddess of flight, wrote: "I believe they wore them as a symbol of their transition."

Nike executives at company headquarters in Beaverton, Oregon, were jolted by the numerous media calls about the sneakers.

"This is a tragedy—it's not about shoes or clothes, it's about a great American tragedy," said Nike spokesman McClain Ramsey.

Marketing experts said even though Nike's swoosh is a cultural icon, the sneaker firm would do best to stay mum. "This has nothing to do with the company," said Seth Siegel, president of Beanstalk Group, a prestigious licensing and marketing firm.

Recalling the infamous mass suicide in Jonestown, Guyana, from poisoned Kool Aid, Siegel said it "didn't reduce Kool Aid sales by one quart, and this will not impact on Nike by a single shoelace."

Mickey Belch, a marketing professor at San Diego State University said many companies would love to be in Nike's sneakers, even with a potential problem.

"I don't think this qualifies as a crisis for Nike, but people will notice," he said.

One consumer in San Diego apparently noticed. He called up a local store and asked whether they carried the Nike brand of "dead men's shoes."

Chapter

10

CYBERSPACE:
CULPRIT OR ACCOMPLICE?

Mopping up after a tragedy the size of the mass suicide in Rancho Santa Fe is a monumental task. There are many loose ends. Some appear as if they may never be tied together.

The wealthy residents of the exclusive community, which fell under the world's microscope on March 26, 1997, surely wanted to get back to normal. Only four days after the discovery of the dozens of poisoned and suffocated bodies, those first steps were quietly taken.

Two local businessmen came forward in an attempt to buy the $1.6 million mansion where the mass suicide took place.

Their plan: Tear the place down and "bring closure to the whole negative event."

Robert Dyson, a local real-estate agent said he brought the two parties together because they had similar intentions for the mansion in the posh suburb.

"Part of the discussion was possibly tearing down this house and starting over again," Dyson said.

The real-estate man said he anticipated things "getting back to normal" in the community, "if we can bring closure to this thing more quickly."

One issue seemed wide open—at least in the eyes of police investigators trying to dot the *i*'s and cross the *t*'s of their probe. That was the true story behind the discovery of the mass suicide by Nick Matzorkis and Rio D'Angelo.

After the two men told their tale of driving down to the house to check on cultists, *New York Post* columnist Steve Dunleavy and *Post* Los Angeles correspondent Brendan Bourne learned some disturbing details of that discovery.

"We know that D'Angelo received letters and tapes . . . heralding the most frightening slumber party in American history at the home of the Heaven's Gate computer cult," Dunleavy wrote.

"Now D'Angelo, a former member of Heaven's Gate, is in Los Angeles, while the tragedy is in San Diego. Why, with vital knowledge of this bone-chilling self-destruction, didn't he alert authorities here?

"Instead, he gets in a car with his Beverly Hills sponsor, a businessman named Nick Matzorkis. Together they drive three hours to the death house while local cops are ignorant of what hell lay inside. It gets worse. D'Angelo goes into the house carrying a video camera in a knapsack. . . . Only after he leaves the mansion of mass suicide does he call the local cops. . . .

"If you or I were in New York and knew about a tragedy in Philadelphia, would we drive down to check it out or would we call the cops? It now emerges that D'Angelo was working with writer/producer Rick Singer on a script called 'Beyond Human: Return of the Next Level.'

"The movie script was bounced by NBC and an unidentified Hollywood producer had also eyeballed the project. But Singer says he got a call from D'Angelo ten days ago. 'He said he wanted to continue pursuing the script and teleplay,' said Singer 'He said, "let's do it." '

"It would be logical to assume that D'Angelo used the camera in his knapsack. And surely, D'Angelo—budding screenwriter that he is—videotaped the bodies for purely investigative reasons to hand over to police to help them in their probe.

"Yeah, right. And I have some swamp land in Florida I'd like to sell you. Lieutenant Jerry Lipscombe, the sheriff heading the investigation in San Diego, said, 'We would like to clear this matter up.' Scriptwriter Singer has been desperately trying to contact D'Angelo, who suddenly has gone underground or is doing some secret negotiating.

"Are we to believe that the frustration level in having a script rejected is so overwhelming that someone sits on knowledge of a looming horror? Please don't tell me that when a studio executive knocks back an idea cynicism boils over to the point where a Hollywood wannabe says to himself: 'You'll be sorry you passed on this one. Wait 'til you find out what happens.'

"We don't truthfully know Mr. D'Angelo's motive. But it is absolutely inexcusable that he would not contact police the moment he had even the slightest suspicion these souls had committed this act. In fact, according to one source, the letter and tapes that D'Angelo had reviewed on Wednesday [March 26] were intended to reach him last Monday [March 24], but the mail was late.

"If the indication of mass suicide had come to him Monday, would some of the victims still be alive? Could someone have headed it off? If this is blind ambition at its Hollywood worst, I'm glad that most of us are a little lazy."

Amid the growing questions Dunleavy raised, ethical questions about the Internet remain.

"Reporters keep calling me and asking if the Internet is to blame for this," said Karen Coyle, western regional director for Computer Users for Social Responsibility in Berkeley, California.

"Of course the Internet isn't to blame for it—any more than the comet is to blame."

Fear of the unknown is only magnifying distrust of cyberspace among computer illiterates, she told the Associated Press.

"Less than half of our households have a computer. Only a third of those log on. So most people see this as being mysterious technology," Coyle said.

And just because Heaven's Gate published its odd statement rants online, doesn't mean there are a lot of readers.

"There's between thirty to forty million web pages out there. They could have done just as well to go out to the San Diego bluffs and thrown a message in a bottle," Coyle said.

Many Internet users are appalled by the uproar. One writer on the WELL, a San Francisco-based Internet service, described a television segment about the issue:

"The computer editor on *Good Morning, America* was BREATHLESS in exclaiming over 10,000 CULT WEBSITES!! and because the Net is global, THEY CAN SET UP THEIR SITES ANYWHERE, and can't be subjected to laws or penalties!!!!! She also had an expert explain how CULT WEBSITES CAN PREY ON PEOPLE!!"

This unwarranted connection between the Internet and cults has frightened some parents beyond reason, said Pam Dixon, author of *Take Charge Computing for Teens and Parents*.

The author said she's been mobbed at the gym by parents who are worried about their children.

"I'm hearing a lot of comments from terrified parents that this is a computer cult. But actually it's not a computer cult. This is a cult who happened to have a website," she said.

"Web pages in and of themselves are not capable of some technological mumbo jumbo whereby they grasp control of your mind and take away your thought processes. The web does not reach out and touch you. You're in control, always."

Online discussions of the controversy raged fast and furious.

"When will this madness end?" pleaded a message dropped into the message group alt.alien.visitors, where UFO believers check in to compare notes. "Those of you who lightly preach this UFO garbage now have blood on your hands."

Replies to that came almost instantly.

"No one ever told these morons in

California to go out and kill themselves to unite with aliens on a ship," read one. "You want blood on hands, talk to the people responsible for alien cover-ups."

Another protested, "Those people had nothing to do with the serious study of the UFO phenomenon. They were a cult, just like any other cult."

Some believers made no apologies. One wrote the depiction of an alien that Heaven's Gate members left behind seemed familiar.

"Having had several close encounters and ET-related experiences myself, I can say that it is indeed pretty representative of the many reports of otherworldly beings," he wrote.

One message on the subject of faith said the suicides offer "proof that smart people can do stupid things if they believe hard enough."

"What poppycock," began a reply. "You all blame God when God never entered into this fiasco at all. In fact, in all the news I have heard, God's name has never once come up. . . . God was far from this event because the participants didn't call on the true God."

It is unclear on where all of the UFO cybercultists stood on the issue of God. But they were sufficiently terrified of outer-space evil.

In one of the strangest aftershocks to come out of the Rancho Santa Fe horror, it was revealed that the group had taken out a multi-million dollar insurance policy against alien abduction, alien impregnation, and death by alien attack.

The annual policy was taken out October 10, 1996, through the underwriting agent Goodfellow Rebecca Ingrams Pearson. The cult moved into its $7,000 a month mansion in Rancho Santa Fe, California, the same month.

The firm, which underwrites on behalf of a group of major insurance companies in the United Kingdom, would have lost $39 million—one million for each cult member—if the coroner's office had been unable to decide the cause of death.

An open verdict would have been an open invitation for the families of the various cult members to pursue the claims in court, noted the underwriters' managing director, Simon Burgess.

"American juries are famous for their perverse judgments," Burgess said. "My belief is that aliens were not involved in these people's death. However, we have to keep an open mind."

A verdict of suicide from the coroner invalidates any claim.

The annual premium for Heaven's Gate, which was listed under the name The Higher Source, the cult's software business arm, in the insurance policy, was $1,000 a year.

The underwriters have insured four-thousand clients worldwide against alien abduction, in addition to insuring several hundred virgins against immaculate conception.

They also offer "Bobbitting" insurance to men who fear being castrated by their wives.

"I'm very happy to part the feeble-minded from their cash," Burgess said.

Epilogue

On TV cop shows, the crime is always committed in the first five minutes and solved by the end of the hour. It never works that way in real life.

Investigations often take years and mysteries remain unsolved for lifetimes. There is rarely a full satisfactory conclusion to any tragedy. There certainly won't be in the case of the Heaven's Gate thirty-nine. There are many loose ends, and the cult's stunning act is still rippling with aftershocks.

Exactly a week after the first group of Applegate's brood began their booze and pills journey to oblivion, the first copycat suicide came.

An aging Grateful Dead fan was found dead with a bag over his head, a triangular scarf shrouding his corpse and a handwritten suicide note saying he intended to join others on a spaceship following the comet Hale-Bopp.

Robert Leon Nichols, fifty-eight, was found just before dawn on March 31, 1997 in his trailer home in a remote canyon in Marysville, California, where he lived alone.

"He had covered his head in a plastic bag, and it appears he had inserted a propane hose underneath the bag and turned on the gas," said Yuba County Undersheriff Gary Finch.

Nichols, in a blue and white T-shirt and blue briefs, also had a multicolored, purple scarf placed from chin-level over his body, Finch said.

A note found near the body stated: "I'm going on the spaceship with Hale-Bopp to be with those who have gone before me."

"He had made a model of a galaxy with a little spaceship out of aluminum foil and hung it from the ceiling so he could view it from the bed," Finch added.

There were some elements in common with the thirty-nine UFO cultists, although he did not have a shaved head and wore different clothing from the other victims.

Nichols "did have a computer, but whether he was linked to [Heaven's Gate], I don't know," Finch said.

Nichols was the author of a book about the Grateful Dead called, *Truckin' with the Grateful Dead in Egypt*.

On the same day, details emerged about what investigators found inside the death house. They showed a blandly normal side to a group of people the nation had branded wackos.

The *San Diego Union-Tribune* revealed that among the products found were: frozen pizzas, strip steaks, Starbucks Java Chip ice cream, 7-Up, Dad's root beer, orange soda, Smucker's grape jelly, Grey Poupon mustard, and a soft drink called "Mango Madness."

Molasses, maple syrup, fresh fruits, and twelve bottles of liquor were discovered.

Wads of cash were found throughout the house totaling $5,400.

Among the books found were: *Your Guide to Self-Care* and *The Reflexology Workout:*

Hand and Foot Massage for Superhealth and Rejuvenation.

The cultists apparently believed in the benefits of vitamins and minerals. Found were: echinacea, brewer's yeast, evening primrose oil, and a vitamin mixture called "Rocket Fuel Action Caps."

The cultists, emphasizing thrift, did most of their shopping at the national food warehouse, Costco.

There were also indications the group watched TV shows that had been approved in advance like *Chicago Hope*. A collection of videotapes found near a giant screen TV are mostly of science-fiction movies and TV shows. Only one general interest movie is among the pile—*The Sound Of Music*, which was said to be Applewhite's favorite movie.

"These weren't people who ate rocks," Susan Jamme, a San Diego County Deputy Public Administrator told the *Union-Tribune*. "There's still some common ground. That was what impacted me: the normalcy."

A document found in one room listed "The 17 Steps," a guide for living geared to new recruits.

They included:

1) Can you follow instructions without adding your own interpretation?
2) Can you deliver instructions as you receive them or do they change according to your computer?
3) Do you participate in inconsiderate conversation, polluting the ears of others while you and your partner work things out?
4) Are you physically clumsy—breaking things because you handle them too harshly or carelessly?
5) Do you halfway complete your task because of your poor standard of what is thorough?
6) Do you put your tasks off—procrastinate?
7) Are your patterns of cleanliness, sensitivity, gentleness, etc., consistent or are they good only when spotlighted?
8) Do you use more of something than is adequate (for example, excessively high cooking flame, more toothpaste than necessary, etc.)?
9) Do you go from one extreme to another—as from undereating to overeating, etc?
10) Are you sensitive when approaching another individual about something you want to

discuss? Do you permit that individual the choice to continue what he is doing, or do you force him to drop it in order to give attention to you? Do you stop and check, or do you assume that what is on your mind is more important than what is on theirs? (Know the difference between your relationship with your teachers and your fellow classmates in this regard.)

11) Do you needlessly ask a question when the answer is obvious or a moment of silent observation would quickly reveal the answer?

12) Are you pushy, aggressive, interfering, or demanding in any way?

13) Has familiarity caused you to become so relaxed with your partners or others that your actions or words don't hold enough restraint?

14) Are you gentle, simple, cautious, and thoughtfully restrained in your steps and all other physical actions and words?

15) Have you outgrown defensiveness and its flip side, martyrdom?

16) Can you understand and review in your mind all the ways in which members of the Next Level are sensitive? If you can, you have no excuse for not working or improving in these areas at all times.

17) When your teachers have asked someone to do a task, and it relates to you, do you start that task and deliver it with as much respect as you would if it came directly from your teachers?

More details of the cult and its doings trickled out day after day.

In San Diego, authorities focused on a couple of possible suspects in their probe into who supplied the cultists with the large supply of prescription pills used in the mass suicide act.

But prosecutors acknowledged even if the culprit or culprits are caught, it is unlikely they would be punished by more than a fine or brief jail term. The pill-pushers' ultimate punishment would be knowing that their supplies were partially responsible for the deaths of thirty-nine highly disturbed people.

On the other side of the world, authorities in Switzerland and France started round-the-clock surveillance of a sun-worshipping cult they believed might be about to pull a similar stunt in the coming months once the constellation formed in a certain pattern.

Appendix

Here is the roll call
of the suicide cult members:

1. Dana Tracey Abreo, 35, of Denver, loyally followed her half-brother, Gary Jordan St. Louis, into Heaven's Gate.
2. Marshall Herff Applewhite, 65, born in Spur, Texas, was the cult co-founder, along with Bonnie Lu Trusdale Nettles, who died in 1985. The charismatic guru's Christian upbringing, obsession with New Age mysticism, and struggle with his sexual identity fueled both the philosophy and final tragedy of Heaven's Gate.
3. Robert John Arancio, 46, of Dallas, handled recruiting business for Heaven's Gate, obtaining business permits in 1993 for Total Overcomers Anonymous.
4. Raymond Alan Bowers, 45, of Jupiter, Florida, a

guitar player who struggled with depression, divorce, and personal tragedies, first met cult members in 1975 but joined them twenty years later.

5. LaDonna Ann Brugato, 40, of Englewood, Colorado, raised with eight brothers and sisters in Newberg, Oregon, was a violinist and computer programmer whose spiritual quest led her to Heaven's Gate.

6. Margaret June Bull, 53, of Ellensburg, Washington, known as "Peggy," joined the group as one of the original followers in the mid 1970s after graduation from the University of Washington and teaching English in Barcelona, Spain.

7. Cheryl Elaine Butcher, 43, of Springfield, Missouri, joined the group in 1976 and helped Arancio handle business matters for the cult.

8. Michael Howard Carrier, 48, listed his address as a Pack 'N Mail store in the Dallas suburb of Richardson, Texas, the same address used by fellow cult members Peggy Bull and Gary St. Louis.

9. Suzanne Sylvia Cooke, 54, was carrying a New Mexico driver's license but had no family there. She lived with other cult members until 1995 on the group's forty-acre youth camp near Mountainair, New Mexico, which the cult dubbed their "earth ship."

10. John M. Craig, 63, of Durango, Colorado, was a successful land developer, former Republican

candidate for local office, husband and father of six when he abruptly rejected it all to join the cult in 1975.

11. Betty Eldrie Deal, 64, was among the older members of the group to die in the mass suicide. She used the Mail Boxes Etc. store in Far North Dallas as her address.

12. Erika Ernst, 40, of Calgary, Canada, was a good student and a fun-loving teen through high school, but after graduating, abruptly left home and joined the cult.

13. Alphonzo Ricardo Foster, 44, of Detroit, was a Michigan native. A passport found on his body at the cult suicide mansion was issued in Los Angeles.

14. Lawrence Jackson Gale, 47, of Lake Forest, California.

15. Darwin Lee Johnson, 42, of Orem, Utah, played in a band called Dharma Combat, which played at local clubs, and wrote songs about death and aliens.

16. Julie LaMontagne, 45, of Brimfield, Massachusetts, was a gifted nurse whose world collapsed with the death of her father in 1975. Shortly after, she met and joined Heaven's Gate.

17. Jacqueline Opal Leonard, 72, of Littleton, Colorado, the oldest among the Heaven's Gate suicide victims, raised two daughters and a son before her restlessness led her to Heaven's Gate.

18. Jeffrey Howard Lewis, 41, a former massage

therapist from San Antonio who joined the group
in the mid 1970s after serving in the Navy in San
Diego, left and rejoined in 1994.

19. Gail Renee Maeder, 28, of Sag Harbor, New York,
wanted to live forever, and Heaven's Gate members promised she would. She left her family and
joined the cult in about 1992.

20. Steven Terry McCarter, 41, listed his address as
Albuquerque, New Mexico.

21. Joel Peter McCormick, 29, of Madison,
Wisconsin, joined the cult in 1994 after a recruit-
ment in Seattle, when the group was known as
Total Overcomers.

22. Yvonne McCurdy-Hill, 39, of Cincinnati, a mother
of five, left her children and job to join, with her
husband Steven, the Heaven's Gate cult in Rancho
Santa Fe. Her husband left, but she stayed on.

23. David Geoffery Moore, 41, of Los Gatos,
California, joined the cult in 1975 as a disaffect-
ed nineteen-year-old, and saw his family only
twice afterward.

24. Nancy Dianne Nelson, 45, of Mesa, Arizona,
worked for an osteopathic surgeon during periods in 1995 and 1996, but told co-workers she
was a nun who lived in a monastery with two men
who were knowledgeable about computers.

25. Norma Jeane Nelson, 59, of North Dallas, told
neighbors she was a crew member on *Star Trek*'s
spaceship.

26. Thomas Alva Nichols, 59, of Arizona, was the

brother of actress Nichelle Nichols, who played
"Lt. Uhura" on the original *Star Trek* television
series.

27. Lindley Ayerhart Pease, 41, of New Hampshire.

28. Lucy Eva Pesho, 63, of Albuqerque, New Mexico.

29. Susan Elizabeth Nora Paup, 54, whose listed
    address was New Mexico, befriended several
    people in the tiny town of Manzano, including
    eleven-year-old Rachel Heard, with whom she
    would talk about school, computers, and UFOs.

30. Margaret Ella Richter, 46, of Oroville, California,
    earned a master's degree in computer science at
    UCLA and soon after joined the cult.

31. Judith Ann Rowland, 50, was from Dallas, Texas.

32. Michael Barr Sandoe, 26, of Boulder, Colorado,
    the senior class president of his Abdingdon,
    Virginia, high school and Army veteran of Desert
    Storm, joined Heaven's Gate after he began trav-
    eling around the country.

33. Brian Alan Schaaf, 40, listed a KOA campground
    in Las Cruces, New Mexico, as his last known
    address.

34. Joyce Angela Skalla, 58, used a Santa Fe, New
    Mexico, address.

35. Gary Jordan St. Louis, 44, of Idaho was brilliant with
    computers, and joined the cult from nearly its start.

36. Susan Frances Strom, 44, was the daughter of
    retired U.S. District Judge Lyle Strom of Omaha,
    Nebraska. She had planned to be a botanist
    before joining the cult in 1975.

37. Denise June Thurman, 44, of Locust Valley, New York, was a happy-go-lucky cheerleader in high school before she turned her attention to the occult. She joined the group in the mid '70s.

38. David Cabot Van Sinderen, 48, of Connecticut, was the son of the former chairman and CEO of Southern New England Telephone Company. His wealth helped finance cult activities, including the purchase of the forty-acre youth camp in New Mexico where cult members lived before moving to Rancho Santa Fe.

39. Gordon Thomas Welch, 50, of Arizona.